D1253942

A Journey of Transformation

A Journey of Transformation

UNIVERSITY OF
SOUTHERN CALIFORNIA
2010–2015

By Rob Asghar

Produced by Epicenter Communications
www.epicenter.com

Printed by The Pace Group
City of Industry, California

ISBN: 978-1-5136-1166-2

First printing: May 2016

Table of Contents

UNIVERSITY OF SOUTHERN CALIFORNIA
1880
PALMAM QUI MERUIT FERAT

This story about the dramatic transformation of USC is at its core a tribute to the dedicated and skillful architects of an ongoing metamorphosis: Elizabeth Garrett, Michael Quick, Al Checcio, Todd Dickey, Tom Jackiewicz, Tom Sayles, Carol Mauch Amir, Pat Haden, Robert Abeles, Lisa Mazzocco, Dennis Cornell, and First Lady Niki C. Nikias. They have inspired our community by demonstrating the fullest potential of great teamwork, in which individual skill and character are magnified, manyfold, by a shared and unshakable resolve to bring to the world something of enduring and limitless value—no matter the obstacles or challenges.

—C. L. Max Nikias, President, USC

ΘΕΜΙΣ ΕΞΑΝΕΓΡΕΣΘΑΙ
TROIHN
University of
Southern California
1880

Introduction

The history of USC may be the quintessential American story: A legend of explorers and pioneers with audacious ambitions and the ability to achieve them. A saga of underdogs who don't simply defy the odds on the way to their goal but rather show deliberate disregard for them. A tale about a community of people with a shared taste for uncertainty, because they believe the greatest opportunities are born of moments that challenge—times of shake-up that embolden us to define and redefine ourselves.

For much of the time since its founding in 1880, the USC story has been beloved by those within its circle of influence—the Trojan Family, as they proudly call themselves—but it was more obscure to those on the outside. In recent decades, however, that began to change. A university that intuitively focused on its own pathway began to gain attention globally.

That USC would gain outside acclaim in any context would be impressive, given its modest roots. What has made its rise over the past five years more remarkable is that it came against the backdrop of tumultuous global change, and accelerated at a time when higher education as a whole was becoming a beleaguered, embattled enterprise. Some skeptics were even predicting that universities as we know them might disappear within a few decades, due to societal, technological, and economic changes.

The USC community anticipated massive, sweeping changes across the American and higher education landscapes. But they also believed that certain universities (especially their own) had a special, even singular, contribution to make in the decades ahead. The Trojan Family stepped forward with a series of bold decisions, commitments, and investments, all undertaken at a time when the traditional order of things was being turned upside down.

Crushed by the pressures of the 2009 recession, most organizations, institutions, and even nations chose to take a cautious route forward, scaling back expectations. By contrast, USC was fueled by a determination to protect its steady rise in recent years, and also to continue to grow, viewing the sweeping change and global uncertainty as a potential opportunity. As other institutions were slowing down, USC was in a position to move ahead of the competition, if it could capitalize swiftly on some key advantages.

Since the school's founding, much of its progress had not occurred in a steady, linear fashion but rather in a number of dramatic bursts and transformations in which its unique character came into contact with a particularly promising set of circumstances. And this time was no different.

LEFT: Judge Robert Maclay Widney, a major force in transforming Los Angeles from a frontier village to a burgeoning world city, labored passionately for years to bring USC into existence. In 2014, the university honored its founder with a statue near the entrance of its University Park Campus to remind new generations of this bold and determined spirit. PREVIOUS PAGE: The Presidential Mace is carried by the head of the Academic Senate during the inaugural procession of a new USC president, to signify the importance of the faculty in the university organization.

The DNA That Drove USC's Growth

All the successes and ongoing commitments of the USC community—in fact, the entire process of metamorphosis by which a humble school has grown into one of the world's most influential—reflect a distinctive institutional DNA.

"Every great institution is the lengthened shadow of a single man," Ralph Waldo Emerson wrote a century and a half ago. "His character determines the character of the organization." Even with the advances of time and technology, and amid dramatic social, economic, and demographic change, the University of Southern California reveals the lengthened shadow and character of its founder, Robert Maclay Widney.

Prior to founding USC, Widney had made a name for himself as a U.S. district judge, an entrepreneur, and a polymath who had been a professor teaching mathematics and law for no pay earlier in his career. While Los Angeles was still a patchwork of dirt roads, farms, and villages, the judge recognized its potential to be an even greater metropolis than its fast-rising cousin to the north, San Francisco. He believed the city could be a global hub for commerce and culture, despite being so far removed from the centers of power in the Atlantic.

Widney would speak to colleagues and friends about Los Angeles as a jewel that needed cutting and polishing. Where others saw a backwater village, he saw an environment that spoke of infinite possibility. At the outset of his presidency, C. L. Max Nikias observed, "Judge Widney saw the majestic mountains with snow in the winter within easy reach. He saw the vast Pacific nearby, which offered open access to a newer world; and a climate designed by heaven itself, offering the unlimited expression of the human mind, body, and spirit. This, he said, is where the next great world city could arise."

Widney then began the process of cutting that jewel, helping bring the railroad to Los Angeles, bringing light and power to the city, and boosting the nascent economy through a new chamber of commerce. As one of Southern California's major architects, however, he recognized that Los Angeles needed a quality university at its core if the region were to manifest its astonishing potential. The financial conditions for such a venture were highly unfavorable when he first announced his goal. Undaunted, however, he spent a decade dreaming, planning, working, sacrificing, and cajoling community support, until the University of Southern California opened its doors in the fall of 1880 to 53 students and 10 teachers.

From its earliest days, the university demonstrated a global character, more committed than its peers to educating students from across the Pacific. Some observers traced this internationalist aspect of its identity to an episode years earlier, in which the judge intervened in an anti-immigrant riot that was typical of the day along the West Coast. At the risk of his own life, the pistol-packing Widney dove into the crowd, fired a bullet in the air to break up the mob, and ushered a number of Chinese immigrants safely from the scene.

"It was at that moment, on that evening that the DNA of USC as a global institution was called into being," President Nikias said at his inaugural address. "In that moment, on that evening, the ethos, the character of USC began to take shape."

Significantly, the university easily could have carried Widney's name. Most private universities bear the monikers of their founders while public schools are more likely to be named for a region. The naming was no accident, however: His new institution was intended from its infancy to have a public mission.

The University of Southern California, Widney's prized achievement on the great Western frontier, reflected a commitment to seeing possibilities where others saw obstacles, and bringing those opportunities to life. Today, its academic community, alumni, and supporters reflect that same determined spirit as new frontiers come into view.

From Regional School to Research Powerhouse

Academically, USC has been on a steady upward climb since Norman H. Topping took on the presidency in 1958. It began that era as a solid, regional school, best known for professional education, and concluded it as a research institution of national distinction—a status that was confirmed when USC was admitted to the prestigious Association of American Universities in 1969.

That pivot, from serving as a regional, professional school to becoming a national research university, was the first major transformation of the modern USC, and it took place in the face of great skepticism. Early in Topping's tenure, *Time* magazine detailed his challenge, claiming that Stanford was "incomparably richer" and that UCLA was "incomparably better." Thus when USC was elected to the AAU five years ahead of crosstown rival UCLA, it was an impressive sign of the Trojan Family's determination to improve academically.

The university underwent another growth spurt in the 1990s, despite a recession and fragile economy, expanding its efforts to recruit top students, support its local community, and improve its campus infrastructure. These accomplishments set the stage for USC's next metamorphosis, which would begin in 2009, during the greatest economic downturn since the Great Depression.

A Difficult Environment for Growth

The year 2009 began with apocalyptic predictions of a worldwide financial crisis. In the wake of the commercial collapse at the end of 2008, trillions of dollars of economic value had evaporated. Some of the mightiest institutions of Wall Street were ghosts haunting the global economy. The unemployment rate was on a steady climb toward the 10 percent mark across the United States by the spring of 2010 and reached 13 percent in Los Angeles County during the same period. Everywhere, simple survival seemed the most plausible goal. Attempts to thrive or excel were dismissed by reasonable people as unrealistic.

Many peer universities were in debt, overextended in expenditures funded by shrunken endowments, or just paralyzed by fear—and therefore unable to invest in any new programs or improvements until the horizon cleared. Such clarity, of course, would not be soon in coming for most institutions across economic sectors. Uncertainty wasn't a phase but rather the new reality. USC adjusted prudently. But it also believed in the future and would budget accordingly.

The university had worked diligently to maintain a solid fiscal foundation and strong cash reserves. Due to the responsible approach of its academic leadership and Board of Trustees, USC was able to move with vigor and make major infrastructure investments even in the valley of the Great Recession. Across the country, municipal and state governments flirted with bankruptcy, Washington was choked under debt, and businesses and other universities looked to cut expenses wherever possible. But USC was in an enviable position, following 129 years of balanced budgets and an approach that was both judicious and entrepreneurial.

In that light, USC's bold expansions and acquisitions during this period symbolized its determination to take control of its own destiny. At the time, some saw these investments as gambles. Yet they reflected the university's belief that—as revolutions took shape in biology and medicine, in globalization, in digital media and online education, and in new forms of the humanities—USC would need to move aggressively to be at the forefront of emerging opportunities.

A Changing of the Guard

The year 2010 also reflected other transitions. USC's 10th president, Steven B. Sample, announced his retirement late that fall, after nearly 19 years in office, during which the university had grown significantly in reputation and productivity. An aggressive and well-publicized national search ensued for a successor who could maintain the school's progress. Edward P. Roski Jr., then board chair, headed a committee composed of trustees and other USC stakeholders, including faculty luminaries such as Kevin Starr, the eminent California historian and former state librarian; Velina Hasu Houston, the internationally renowned playwright; and Warren Bennis, widely considered one of the most prominent leadership experts of his generation. Bennis often spoke about how great helmsmen are characterized by "unwarranted optimism," even in the most trying of circumstances and searing of crucibles.

Enter Nikias, USC's provost during the previous five years of rapid growth. The search committee, after an exhaustive examination of 75 candidates from across the country, unanimously recommended to the full Board of Trustees in March 2010 that Nikias be named USC's 11th president.

Members of the committee expressed surprise at the bold academic agenda Nikias set forth in the search interview process to elevate the university from a position of strength to a premier standing in the world of higher education. Some aspects of the plan were sweeping while others were bluntly specific. Nikias argued that USC should not be content to make incremental progress. Rather, he said, it should seize a once-in-a-century chance to achieve an undisputed elite status, which would allow its academic community to bring its unique combination of talents to bear on the challenges of the coming era. A window of opportunity had opened, he said, but it would remain so for only a few years. USC had to move quickly and decisively.

The three keys, he said, involved faculty, medicine, and money. Nikias emphasized that USC needed to dramatically strengthen the profile of its faculty, especially in emerging disciplines. He argued that the institution also had to pivot academically in order to be a major player in the global revolutions happening in medicine, biology, and healthcare. These initiatives would require billions of dollars in short order, and so he called for a fast-track plan for a historic fundraising campaign that would boost USC's endowment.

It is worth noting that an internal succession of a president is relatively rare within higher education. While corporations often groom candidates from within their organization to succeed a celebrated CEO, universities tend to turn to the outside in search of their next leader. In USC's case, the elevation of Nikias to the presidency symbolized a desire for continuity—not the sort of continuity that merely preserves the status quo, however, but rather a commitment to keeping the university's pedal to the floor and even accelerating its pace.

A Snapshot of Dramatic Progress

Perhaps Nikias's most valuable asset for the job ahead was his ability to give passionate expression to the USC community's far-reaching ambition. Indeed, the school's longtime members and leaders weren't content to see it continue on a gradually rising path. Rather, they responded to the idea that their university was undergoing a metamorphosis—a stage of rare transformation, in which its particular traits could give birth to something previously unseen, and of the highest value. Energized by this renewed vision, they moved forward with both determination and optimism.

By 2015, even as the specter of the recession lingered, it had become clear that the changes begun in 2009 and 2010 were approaching a major next stage of development. This evidence came in several forms and arenas.

Support for the USC Mission

The university publicly announced a fundraising campaign in 2011, amid the economic softness of a jobless recovery. The total goal, $6 billion within eight years, exceeded any campaign previously announced by any university. Many higher education observers wondered if the Trojans could raise this ambitious sum. Yet, as trustees and donors paved the way with major early gifts, USC reached the $4.5 billion mark in the first five years. About half of the money came from 27 transformative gifts of $25 million or more, with four of those at the level of $100 million or more.

More than 290,000 donors have advanced USC's *Fas Regna Trojae* campaign, with gifts of every size making powerful statements about the breadth and depth of support that exists around the world. Approximately 60 percent of the money raised came from non-alumni, a striking sign of the university's ability to find support beyond the Trojan Family.

The Rise of USC's Faculty

The foundation of the university's excellence, its faculty, was solidified and reinforced. USC recruited top scholars in every key discipline—including the arts and humanities, social sciences and professions, science and technology—from leading institutions such as Harvard, Caltech, Stanford, Northwestern, the Cleveland Clinic, UCLA, Michigan, UC San Diego, UC Berkeley, and the Scripps Institute.

A Uniquely Gifted Student Population

USC's student body—already one of the most gifted and broadly talented in the world—grew further in stature. By 2015, it could be viewed accurately as a hybrid of the populations of premier research institutions, such as Caltech and Stanford, and the world's greatest arts conservatories.

Average undergraduate SAT scores rose to the 95th percentile nationally, up from the 50th percentile just a generation earlier. The university received 53,000 applications in 2015 for only 2,700 freshman seats, and its 18 percent admissions rate was the lowest in its history. Graduation rates had risen to an impressive 92 percent, a crucial sign that USC was increasingly able to offer a fulfilling experience to first-rate students.

Nearly a quarter of the school's freshmen were now from underrepresented ethnic backgrounds, and by 2015, it ranked third among private American universities in total Pell Grant recipients. Once seen as economically exclusive, this private university was now more inclusive than even its public peers in enrolling qualified students from every background.

A Bold Move into the New Age of Medicine

The evolution of the overall university was symbolized by the changes in its academic medical and health enterprise. As these fields emerged as the chief intellectual disciplines of the 21st century, USC's leaders moved to ensure that its faculty and students were in a position to play a leadership role in a global health revolution. The university radically escalated its commitment to these fields—once again using interdisciplinary strengths that spanned both its campuses to accomplish quickly what traditional pacesetters in these areas could not.

Pioneering Research

USC's research mission was thriving, as faculty and students stormed some of the most important academic frontiers of the coming decades. At the graduate and doctoral levels, the university became a magnet for more talented students than ever before. USC's faculty was able to race past the competition because of its particularly strong emphasis on cross-disciplinary research. For instance, its unique ability to combine social sciences, technology, and the arts allowed it to move to the forefront in informatics and digital media at a time when few other domains were more important to economic and social progress.

A Brighter Spotlight on the Arts

The university community viewed its unusually wide array of internationally recognized arts programs as nothing less than a "secret weapon" that set it apart from peer research universities. The newly endowed Glorya Kaufman School of Dance joined USC's five other world-class independent art schools, in architecture, cinematic arts, fine arts and design, music, and theater, providing the university with an even broader foundation in the creative and performing arenas. The USC Jimmy Iovine and Andre Young Academy for Arts, Technology and the Business of Innovation, established in 2013, recruits multitalented students who are poised to make magic happen at the boundaries of creative and technical disciplines. And the Visions & Voices arts and humanities initiative allowed students from every field of study to connect with dynamic cultural presentations.

Athletics: Renewing the Trojan Spirit

The university's unrivaled student-athlete tradition, which binds the hearts of Trojans around the world, went through a great renewal, at a moment when intercollegiate athletics at the national level were being tested in a crucible of change. Persevering through five years of the most disproportionately tough sanctions ever placed on an NCAA program, USC's short-handed football team maintained a high level of excellence, achieving as good a record as rival Notre Dame over the same period—and a better record than competitors UCLA and Texas.

The 2012 Summer Olympics in London were the most successful games ever for Trojan athletes, resulting in 25 medals. The university built major athletic facilities, including the John McKay Center and the Uytengsu Aquatics Center, and renovated existing ones. It also took on a 98-year master lease for the Los Angeles Memorial Coliseum, ensuring that the home of the Trojans (and one of the nation's most venerable sporting venues) would be restored to glory.

Guiding the Online Education Revolution

USC's faculty created the world's first sustainable model for online higher education, a template that others would soon begin to use. While some experts had predicted that the ballyhooed online revolution would deliver undergraduate education globally at little or no expense, and possibly even make college campuses obsolete, USC developed an approach that did not succumb to the hype or backlash that plagued creators of other strategies. By the end of 2014, the university had some 8,700 tuition-paying students in 40 countries enrolled in online graduate and continuing education programs, with revenues reaching $150 million—more than at any peer institution.

Building the Campus Infrastructure

Major renovations and improvements to USC's infrastructure symbolized the academic progress under way throughout the university. New facilities such as Dr. Verna and Peter Dauterive Hall, Wallis Annenberg Hall, the Ronald Tutor Campus Center, and the Engemann Student Health Center were outward manifestations of USC's many rapid advancements. And community residents and the university celebrated the groundbreaking of the $650 million USC Village project, the largest economic redevelopment undertaking in the history of South Los Angeles.

A Truly Global University

As globalization became the inexorable reality of our times, every major university sought ways to become more international. USC moved closer, however, to being the first truly global university by capitalizing aggressively on natural assets such as its location at the hub of the Pacific Rim and its traditional role as the home to more international students than any other American university. By 2015, USC had established a permanent presence in key cities across Asia and Latin America, which would nurture academic partnerships and student recruitment efforts.

Extending the New Traditions of the Trojan Family

The Trojan Family, now 350,000 members strong, developed a host of new traditions in addition to the most enduring ones of the past. Each Thanksgiving, the president and first lady hosted at their home hundreds of students with families too far to visit during the holiday. Nikias also created a regular tea-and-conversation program, through which he could personally connect with small groups representing a cross section of USC's 43,000 students, and invite them to share thoughts, concerns, and ideas regarding the life of the university.

A Continuing Transformation

USC's substantial progress was obvious to observers of the higher education scene. A front-page *Los Angeles Times* feature in June 2015 trumpeted the university's rapid gains in academic and financial strength; and it credited them to the president's vision and drive, along with the zeal of the Trojan Family faithful.

But the mood of the university community remained one of focused resolve, rather than self-congratulation. After all, its goal wasn't incremental progress but rather a broad transformation of USC into an institution that could set the standard for decades and generations to come. Any such metamorphosis—whether we speak of a flower in mid-bloom or a large institution undergoing change—is a delicate and complex matter, consisting of myriad transitions and improvements. The milestones the university achieved in this short time period serve as a foretaste of things to come and a reminder that the journey will continue for many more years.

Chapter 1

A New Vision for the Future

The Inauguration of C. L. Max Nikias

In October 2010, the University of Southern California hosted several days of formal and informal events to celebrate the inauguration of C. L. Max Nikias as the 11th president in its 130-years-and-counting history. "This wasn't simply about installing a new USC president," said then-Board Chair Edward P. Roski Jr., who had led the search committee. "This was a once-in-a-generation event, a chance for the university community to take stock of what it had achieved and what it wanted to achieve in the years ahead."

Nikias officially took office on August 3, 2010; the weekend-long celebration that formally inducted him into his new role took place two months later. Performances and lectures leading up to the inauguration spanned the arts, humanities, education, and globalization, including a Visions & Voices Signature Event with public radio's Ira Glass.

The highlight of inauguration eve, Thursday, October 14, was a special performance by the USC Thornton Symphony, conducted by former Thornton School of Music dean Larry Livingston. The orchestra performed Tchaikovsky's *Rococo Variations*, Wagner's *Overture to Die Meistersinger*, and Respighi's *Pines of Rome*. Notably, the evening featured the world premiere of a work by Thornton faculty member Erica Muhl composed specially for the inauguration, titled "Burn the Box." Muhl said the piece had been inspired by a comment she heard Nikias make, in which he quoted management expert Tom Peters on the need not only to "push the envelope" or "think outside the box" but to "rip up the envelope and burn the box." She said, "I wanted the work to be a celebration for President Nikias but also descriptive of this exciting new period in USC's history."

The following morning brought events to a climax with the formal inauguration ceremony, which drew 10,000 guests, including members of the Trojan Family, the local community, and leaders from government, industry, and academia. Roski served as master of ceremonies for the occasion.

C. L. Max Nikias spent nearly two decades on the USC faculty, including five years as provost, before assuming the university's presidency. On October 15, 2010, some 10,000 members of the Trojan Family, along with elected officials and representatives from the national higher education and local communities, convened to formally inaugurate the university's 11th president.

The event began with the traditional procession of academic groups. For the first time, students carried flags from their own nations, more than 120 altogether, symbolizing the international character of the university. The Trojan Marching Band unveiled a work composed for the day by award-winning Thornton School of Music alumnus Andrew Norman. Entitled "...toward sunrise and the prime of light...," the piece was inspired by a passage from Virgil's *Aeneid,* to which Nikias would make significant reference in his inaugural address.

Los Angeles mayor Antonio Villaraigosa and UC Santa Barbara chancellor Henry Yang spoke at the ceremony, praising the leadership ability of Nikias and calling the USC community forward to seize its opportunities. The featured guest speaker was John Hood, the former vice chancellor of Oxford University and president and chief executive officer of the Robertson Foundation in New York. He discussed the evolving nature of the university's mission, even as its character remains unchanged. "I assure you, it is USC's essential character today and in the future that has been consuming President Nikias's thinking and will guide his journey."

In Nikias, the university had found a leader with deep roots, going back two decades in the USC community, who cherished the institution's character and ambitions. Yet it had also found a person with a clear and compelling vision for how it could continue to move forward toward a powerful transformation—one that was under way but far from complete.

Deeply Rooted in the Trojan Family

Nikias, with his wife, Niki, and their two daughters, Georgiana and Maria, had first come to USC in 1991. His initial role at the university was as a professor of electrical engineering.

Within a few years, he was charged with leading the effort to compete with the nation's top universities for the opportunity to host a national multimedia research center funded by the National Science Foundation. Given that global research powerhouses like UC Berkeley and Columbia made this a major priority of their own, for USC this was a pivotal early test of its ability to "punch above its weight" academically. In 1996, victory came to Nikias and the large team he assembled, spanning both academia and industry. Their

The new president and first lady, Max and Niki C. Nikias, partners for four decades, share a quiet moment in the president's office before the inaugural procession begins. In the next chapter of their journey, they would devote much of their time together serving hundreds of thousands of members of the worldwide Trojan Family.

proposal was ranked the best of the 117 that were submitted, and Nikias became the founding director of the NSF-funded Integrated Media Systems Center at USC Viterbi.

In 2001, he was named dean of USC's engineering school, and had great success in building its academic and financial strength. One of his notable accomplishments was working with technology pioneer Andrew Viterbi and his wife, Erna, to establish a $52 million gift that would place their name upon the school in perpetuity.

Nikias succeeded Lloyd Armstrong as provost for the university in 2005. As USC's second-ranking officer, he became the de facto COO of a vast city within a city, a multibillion-dollar amalgam of major technical institutes, liberal arts colleges, arts conservatories, hospitals, and laboratories; living and dining facilities for 43,000 students; and the meeting place and spiritual home of 350,000 alumni. He had direct oversight of the university's 19 professional schools, clinical-care enterprises, admissions, and student life.

During his tenure as provost, Nikias launched several academic centers and innovative programs in the arts. He was instrumental in bringing Trustee Steven Spielberg's Shoah Foundation Institute and its vast video archive of

more than 53,000 testimonies of Holocaust survivors to USC. He also created Visions & Voices, a campus-wide initiative to make the university's world-class arts programs of maximum educational benefit to students in every field.

However, even more vital to USC's health and growth was his financial stewardship. Nikias took on budgetary responsibility for the full university—a role he had previously assumed for the Viterbi School as dean but one that was

On the eve of the inauguration, Nikias greets his mentor, Dr. John H. Siegel, from the department of surgery at SUNY Buffalo. Siegel arranged the NIH-funded research assistantship that originally allowed the Nikiases to come to America as graduate students in January 1979.

Dennis Cornell, standing next to Nikias, joined the president's cabinet in 2010 as chief of staff, following decades of service to USC as its chief of protocol, head of university events, and a faculty member at the USC School of Dramatic Arts.

unlike most provosts at similar institutions, as well as previous holders of the office at USC. Historically, this university-wide responsibility was held jointly by the chief financial officer and the senior vice president for administration and finance. In this role, Nikias strategically invested resources in academic growth and improving student and faculty recruitment while simultaneously building up USC's working capital for a rainy day.

When that day came, in the form of a global economic typhoon at the end of 2008, the university had $500 million in cash reserves—more than it had ever enjoyed in the past, and a level that still exists today. This gave USC an enviable ability to venture in new directions while other schools holed up and held on for dear life. A number of peer universities may have been far richer, but they were also financially extended in ways that left them little room to maneuver, never mind to improve or grow. Provost Nikias believed USC would now be in a position for academic evolution, or even revolution, at this labile moment within higher education.

Trustees who were involved in the presidential search would later remark that Nikias's vision for the university's future—along with his deep understanding of its community and his successes at every level—made him by far the most compelling contender for the office.

Accelerating the Pace of the Metamorphosis

USC's presidential inauguration and celebration of the future came at a time of global economic and societal flux. When he came to deliver his address on that October morning, Nikias—known as a warm, gregarious person of unbounded optimism—began by acknowledging the situation head-on. He told the audience:

> One of the few certainties in our world is that as the pace of change accelerates, the level of uncertainty will increase. But what is uncertainty? In the proper light, uncertainty is the beginning of adventure! And the ability to turn uncertainty into adventure, into a magnificent journey forward, is what defines a Trojan. It is what it means to be a Trojan.

He also assured the Trojan Family that if USC could be bold and aggressive in that difficult climate, it could make incredible progress in the next few years. He reasoned that other universities would inevitably backslide during that same period, and that most would do well simply to maintain their position. In relative and absolute terms, this reality gave USC a once-in-a-lifetime opportunity to build a global institution of unsurpassed excellence and influence across its vast spectrum of intellectual disciplines, spanning the arts and humanities, sciences, technology, medicine, and the professions.

Just as important, he pointed out that new progress would be made at the intersections of these disciplines, where intellectual cross-fertilization occurs. While interdisciplinarity was now widely discussed in the higher education community as an important key to innovation, Nikias emphasized that USC was uniquely able to pursue it.

A Promethean Role in the Age of the Pacific

A striking aspect of the vision Nikias described for the university in his inaugural address was the way in which USC, by coming into its own, could play a role parallel to that of one of the world's most respected institutions. "While USC imitates no one," he said, "I do believe USC has the chance to serve as an intellectual engine in this century, in much the way Oxford University emerged earlier as the intellectual engine of the British Empire and commonwealth nations."

Georgiana (center) and Maria (right) Nikias have both participated in academic processions marking their own receipt of USC degrees. They return to take part in a different academic procession: installing their father as USC's president. In the foreground is John Hood, former vice chancellor of Oxford University, who offered the keynote address.

The reason, he said, was that the much-anticipated Age of the Pacific had finally arrived. The university's Southern California setting was no longer a dusty frontier ignored by the elites on both sides of the Atlantic. The eyes of the top institutions of the previous century now looked west, to consider a new world. He argued that USC shouldn't hope to be merely a part of this Pacific surge but should aspire to lead it:

> As our world today is shifting away from an Atlantic to a Pacific century, USC is better positioned than anyone else to lead this

change. To become the intellectual and cultural and spiritual fabric of a world that is tied to the Age of the Pacific. To become the foremost laboratory of experimentation of "East-West" ideas, in scholarship and the arts and media and journalism and culture. To become the campus where the influencers of the Pacific age will be educated, shaped, and molded.

"Destiny has dealt a favorable hand to USC," he went on to say. "Let us play this out wisely."

The new president and first lady walk forth in the processional, from the Bovard Administration Building, toward USC's stately Doheny Memorial Library, and into Alumni Park for the formal ceremony.

Peter Conti, then president of USC's Academic Senate, leads the procession, wielding the mace of the university to symbolize the central role of the faculty. Following him are the deans of USC schools and delegations representing a variety of stakeholders in the life of the university.

What It Means to Be a Trojan

For nearly a century prior to Nikias's inauguration, USC had collectively called itself the Trojans. The name was inspired in 1912 by the *Los Angeles Times* sports writer Owen Bird, who praised the university's undermanned track team for fighting like Trojans, despite the odds.

But, as Providence would have it, it would take USC's 11th president, a man of Greek Cypriot origin and a devoted Greco-Roman classicist, to spell out the deepest meaning of what it meant to be a Trojan. And he used his inaugural address to do so, in memorable fashion:

> As a child, I grew up reading the various legends of the ancient City of Troy. The Trojan empire represented a classical tradition of excellence and purity of purpose. The Trojans represented a tradition of ongoing renewal. They renewed their great society many times, each time achieving a new glory for themselves and for those who would come after them. No one worked harder than the Trojans, no one was more determined than the Trojans. And their will toward greatness could even bend the will of the gods in their favor.

Moment of transition: USC's 10th president, Steven B. Sample (right), congratulates his successor, C. L. Max Nikias, after placing the Presidential Medallion upon his shoulders.

With the formal ceremony concluded and the recessional from Alumni Park under way, the new president and first lady greet well-wishers.

So in this moment of our renewal, allow me to look back to an epic story told 2,000 years ago, by the Roman poet Virgil. In the epic poem *The Aeneid,* Virgil chronicled the story of the Trojan hero Aeneas. Aeneas and the Trojans responded with courage when fate made it clear that the Trojans would have to seek their destiny beyond the walls of the old City of Troy. So the Trojans set sail and navigated the uncertainties of their times. They navigated their way through raging winds and waters. They navigated through the extreme anger of gods and spirits. They navigated through the full catalog of uncontrollable monsters of antiquity.

Aeneas and the Trojans would reach their destination, where they would lay the cornerstone for a new City of Troy. This Troy would grow into the great city of Rome. Rome—the home to the mightiest and most enduring of all empires. That was the destiny the Trojans began to claim, when they moved from what was comfortable and familiar, when they were willing to lose sight of their native shores and undertake a great journey. Virgil's *Aeneid* makes the timely eternal, and the eternal timely.

The story could not be understood, Nikias said, without realizing that it comes to its conclusion only when the Trojans lay the cornerstone for the mightiest of all empires. The president now sought to bring that same sense of destiny to a broad academic community, one which would fight on to achieve its noble goals in a host of arenas.

Toward the end of his inaugural address, Nikias drew his audience's eyes to that most beloved USC icon, the statue of Tommy Trojan standing guard across from Alumni Park. At the base of the statue was an inscription that could easily be overlooked.

"You may need your glasses to read these lines," Nikias said, "which are

inscribed in very small letters: 'Here are provided seats of meditative joy, where shall rise again the destined reign of Troy.'"

This destined reign of Troy—or *fas regna Trojae* in the original Latin—would become an increasingly important theme in Nikias's presidency. In the time of *The Aeneid,* it required a mighty, collective effort to establish the new Troy, which would ultimately grow into Rome. Amid the uncertainty of 2010, Nikias offered a vision for USC's Trojan Family, if it could summon the same mighty effort:

> The destined reign of Troy is an intellectual community that has achieved undisputed elite status—at the very epicenter of global

President and First Lady Nikias and Trustee Edward P. Roski Jr., after the formal ceremony. Roski, a USC alumnus, chaired the 2009–2010 presidential search committee that recommended the election of Nikias to the full Board of Trustees.

Trustee and alumnus Andrew Viterbi warmly greets his longtime friend and colleague. To honor Nikias's Cypriot origins, Viterbi donned the academic garb he had worn earlier that year when receiving an honorary degree from the University of Cyprus. The digital communications pioneer, with his wife, Erna, endowed the USC Viterbi School of Engineering during Nikias's tenure as dean of the school.

> influence. When you are there, there is no doubt, there is no argument, you belong within the pantheon of world-class universities. There is no question that your voice shall be heard, and that your ideas are received. And there is no limit on the impact USC is able to make upon the world.

The inaugural ceremony and the announcement of USC's lofty goals were punctuated with fireworks—not just the usual kind, but also with some bold acts by two trustees who wanted to give tangible expressions of support for the university's renewed vision.

After Nikias had finished his address, Trustee Ming Hsieh stepped forward to pledge to advance USC's work in health and medicine with a $50 million gift to establish an institute that would bring together engineers, physicians, and scientists to find new ways to fight cancer.

Board chair and master of ceremonies Edward Roski then returned to the podium to announce a second $50 million gift, this one from Trustee Wallis Annenberg, to build a futuristic facility for the USC Annenberg School for Communication and Journalism.

USC TROJANS
1928 1931 1932 1939 1962 1967 NATIONAL CHAMPIONS 1972 1974 1978 2003 2004
'23 '30 '32 '33 '39 '40 '44 '45 '46 '48 '53 '55 '63 '67 '68 '69 '70 '73 ROSE BOWLS '74 '75 '77 '79 '80 '85 '88 '89 '90 '96 '04 '06 '07 '08 '09

Just call him "Max": The famed Trojan Marching Band, at USC's football game the next day against the California Bears, emphatically spells out its support for the new president. Above, the president and first lady cheer on the Trojans, who won 48–14.

Calling the two gifts a "strong vote of confidence in our new president," Roski said, "One hundred million dollars. I'd say that's getting off to a good start, Max!"

It was a good start, indeed. But as Nikias himself had emphasized to the audience that day, the road ahead was not to be seen as an easy one. Endurance would be as important as enthusiasm for the upcoming journey, if the USC community was to begin together a new era of growth and transformation.

UNIVERSITY OF SOUTHERN CALIFORNIA
1880

The Destined Reign of Troy

Inaugural Address, October 15, 2010

There is no adequate way to convey the sense that fills me, standing before you, the women and men of the university that I love, and knowing the profound responsibility with which I have been entrusted.

I shall forever be grateful to all of today's representatives who have offered support and encouragement on behalf of the USC community—our trustees, faculty, students, staff, and our alumni, as well as our friends in the community of Los Angeles and the community of American higher education.

I thank each person in attendance today, for sharing with my family and with the Trojan Family this special moment in our history.

But first, I must take a moment to acknowledge my wife Niki, our first lady of USC. Today is an unusual milestone for Niki and me on our shared journey. Our voyage began more than a third of a century ago, when we decided to pursue the dream of a better life through better education, and to cast our fate across the Atlantic, toward America.

Coming from so far away, so many years ago, we could not have imagined how wonderful this American journey would be. I became forever fascinated by the intellectual electricity and the openness you could find only at an American university. And, far from ending up lost, we were carried along on the gracious currents of goodness. We were welcomed and embraced, and we were given opportunities that we never could have found elsewhere.

So, on our journey, at last, two decades ago, Niki and I reached our Ithaca, by which I mean Los Angeles, and our home at USC. Georgiana and Maria, our daughters, were small children when we arrived in Los Angeles. Our family quickly became a Trojan Family, and we were grateful for how the larger Trojan Family embraced us. We have a passion for this university, and for what it represents. Our family is rooted here. We have immersed ourselves in USC's rich intellectual and cultural life. And we have cherished the great Trojan athletic spirit, which serves as the glue for our worldwide Trojan Family.

Niki and I believe that, when you have been given so much, you have a debt to repay. Because we are grateful, grateful beyond words, we look for ways to repay that debt. One way is by ensuring that the best students—from here and from abroad—can pursue their dreams here, the dreams that are made possible by the best education.

We have always believed that education is the Great Equalizer for a society. Education lifts up the weak from despair, and it teaches humility to the mighty. Education is what helps us to be fully human and to appreciate the full range of human experience in our own life. Education is what expands our lives to be as vast as the frontiers of the cosmos and the edges of eternity, and yet it gives us deep insight into the fleeting moments of our own inner existence.

Working together to take USC higher, to the undisputed mountaintop, will be our payment on the debt—our debt to this great nation, to the Trojan Family, and to Steve and Kathryn Sample.

In a coincidence of fate, one that the playwrights of antiquity would have loved, we never could have imagined that Steve Sample, the man who signed my diploma and Niki's diploma in Buffalo, New York, would be such a wonderful mentor. Steve and Kathryn Sample demonstrated for us what it means to dedicate oneself fully to the demands of the presidency.

The best way to honor their legacy is to take this great university they have given us and make it even greater. Indeed, we owe it to future generations of Trojans to do so. We owe it to our children and grandchildren.

Uncertainty as Opportunity

Today we live in a time of great anxiety. The wisest experts can find little agreement on what the future holds for our society. Regarding the next 20 years, there is no consensus on

- *Which institutions and industries will exist in their current form; or*
- *Whether the career or specialty that a person has chosen today will still exist then; or*
- *Whether the ways in which we interact and communicate will resemble the way we do so now; or*
- *Whether the United States can remain at the forefront of technology, commerce, and culture.*

Universities have their own special concerns. The college-age population will decrease in size in the next few years, making competition for students even harder. Universities will be under added pressure to make college affordable for capable young people from every background.

One of the few certainties in our world is that, as the pace of change accelerates, the level of uncertainty will increase.

But what is uncertainty? In the proper light, uncertainty is the beginning of adventure! And the ability to turn uncertainty into adventure, into a magnificent journey forward, is what defines a Trojan. It is what it means to be a Trojan.

As a child, I grew up reading the various legends of the ancient City of Troy. The Trojan Empire represented a classical tradition of excellence and purity of purpose. The Trojans represented a tradition of ongoing renewal. They renewed their great society many times, each time achieving a new glory for themselves and for those who would come after them. No one worked harder than the Trojans, no one was more determined than the Trojans. And their will toward greatness could even bend the will of the gods in their favor.

So in this moment of our renewal, allow me to look back to an epic story told two thousand years ago, by the Roman poet Virgil. In the epic poem The Aeneid, *Virgil chronicled the story of the Trojan hero Aeneas. Aeneas and the Trojans responded with courage when fate made it clear that the Trojans would have to seek their destiny beyond the walls of the old City of Troy. So the Trojans set sail and navigated the uncertainties of their times. They navigated their way through raging winds and waters. They navigated through the extreme anger of gods and spirits. They navigated through the full catalog of uncontrollable monsters of antiquity. Aeneas and the Trojans would reach their destination, where they would lay the cornerstone for a new City of Troy. This Troy would grow into the great city of Rome. Rome—the home to the mightiest and most enduring of all empires. That was the destiny the Trojans began to claim, when they moved from what was comfortable and familiar, when they were willing to lose sight of their native shores and undertake a Great Journey. Virgil's* Aeneid *makes the timely eternal, and the eternal timely.*

For this university and for our Trojan Family, our own quest for undisputed elite status could be likened to the voyage of Aeneas. It means the difference between being a "hot" and "up-and-coming" university and being undisputedly one of the most elite and influential institutions in the world! A Great Journey awaits us, and on the other side of the adventure lies our destiny.

My own commitment to you is to clear and lead the way for you as we move forward in this Great Journey.

My commitment to you is to champion your cause in every way, around the nation, around the Pacific Rim, in our nation's capital, in Sacramento, in City Hall, in Indianapolis, and wherever else you need allies.

My commitment to you is to point the world's attention to you, as the women and men who will drive society forward.

My commitment to you is to seek the outside resources and raise the funds USC needs, relentlessly, in order to secure academic excellence for the long haul.

My own commitment to you, and that of my administration, is to run the next marathon at a sprinter's pace. We can make incredible progress in just the next few years!

The Five Priorities of USC's Great Journey

Look how far USC has already come. Consider the small and dusty village that represented Los Angeles and USC in 1880. Look at USC's breathtaking rise in the past two decades. Look at the impact we are now able to make because of the lofty position USC has now claimed.

And now, consider the voyage that still lies ahead.

USC's Great Journey will be different from that of other great universities. And USC's role and identity will be different, once we have reached our destination of undisputed elite status.

Let's make no mistake about it: When it comes to doing good for the world, we believe there is a USC way of doing it. This way is entrepreneurial, imaginative, collaborative, ethical, adaptable, and global. We must place this USC stamp on the intellectual and the social revolutions that lie ahead.

The Great Journey for USC is ultimately about five priorities, which are ultimately embodied in people—the very best people.

First, our Great Journey requires that we achieve a critical mass of the world's most brilliant faculty minds—the most productive and renowned intellectual giants of our generation. Transformational faculty whose reputation for productivity will place USC at the vanguard of every intellectual revolution. This requires that we give our faculty the resources to fulfill their immense potential. This requires that we aggressively recruit new, interdisciplinary superstars who can raise the skyline of our entire academic community.

Second, we must build an unsurpassed network and |quality of young women and men capable of leading the future—students from all 50 states and from across the Pacific Rim—from East Asia and South Asia and India and the emerging economies of Latin America. And for these students, let us make them a pledge. Let us pledge to build for them a curriculum of unique quality and variety, a rich curriculum that presents them with an unsurpassed range of choices, so that they may explore and discover their strengths and their passions.

Let us pledge to ensure for them unlimited social and cultural opportunities that prepare them for life in the new world that awaits them. May we do this through the most engaging environment for learning and for living. May we do this through an experience that immerses them in the arts and through emerging forms of media literacy. May we do this through an experience that immerses them in the very manner of global diversity, which they must learn to understand and to navigate.

In this way, our students will become world citizen leaders, who can find and open new doors, and who can support one another as a worldwide Trojan Family.

For our third priority, our Great Journey demands that our academic community be equipped to explore and to lead the major new frontiers of human progress:

- *In the arts and humanities that infuse our society with imagination, creativity, and wisdom;*
- *In the social sciences and the professions that organize and mobilize our human society;*
- *In engineering and sciences that reach out across the cosmos;*
- *In the digital media that enable human interaction, entertainment, news, and information;*
- *And in medicine and biology and biotech, which together represent the most promising frontier of our young century.*

Fourth, our Great Journey demands that our Health Sciences Campus and the University Park Campus represent one unified USC. Though they are seated at different ends of downtown Los Angeles, they must have one character and one shared identity. Our faculty and students must bridge the distance between the two campuses, with interdisciplinary work that provides USC with a crucial leadership asset as biology and medicine emerge as the queen of the sciences in this century.

The residential and academic environment on both campuses must be perfected—for undergraduate students, for graduate and PhD students, and for faculty masters. USC should be an around-the-clock living and learning community, a rare social and physical environment that radiates academic energy.

And our fifth priority must be to recognize the surrounding community as the jewel that it is. The 224 languages that are spoken in this city, and the 115 nations represented today on this campus, are distinctly representative of a new world that is tilted toward the civilizations of the Pacific. A simple drive up Vermont Avenue does not simply show us a city. It displays to us the extraordinary span of Pacific Rim, in microcosm. We will embrace this community as a unique social laboratory, within the context of our mission in education, social-science scholarship, healthcare, and public service.

This local microcosm of a new, global reality will help USC guide the tectonic shift that is already underway in this world. The old City of Troy was in the heart of the great Mediterranean civilization, which long represented the center of gravity for much of human society's development. The center of gravity gradually moved westward. And for the past two centuries, we have lived in the Age of the Atlantic. Many institutions gained prominence by their proximity and relevance to this region.

For most of this time, Southern California was a far-off outpost in the American West. Yet for decades or even centuries to come, this remote Western outpost will be the hub connecting the United States to a world that is centered around the Pacific Rim. Cultures and ideas will collide in this global Age of the Pacific in ways we cannot yet predict. Who will have the ability to lead, to bring shape to the changes?

A story comes to mind about the chief founder of USC,

Robert Maclay Widney, who would also become USC's first chair of the Board of Trustees. He personally wrote the USC articles of incorporation. In the 1870s, Robert Widney had a strong desire to establish a great university in Southern California. He had accomplished much in his life. He was a U.S. district judge. He helped bring the Southern Pacific Railroad to L.A. He organized the first chamber of commerce and the city's first light and power company. But he wasn't yet able to build a university that could shape the future of this region. For 10 years, Judge Widney struggled. Yet he did not give up.

During that same time, the American West was struggling with an early collision of cultures: Anti-Chinese sentiment ran high across the West. Jealousy, economic fears, and labor disputes fanned the flames of violence and murder. One night, anti-Chinese riots broke out in Los Angeles. Deadly mobs took to the streets. And at a moment of high fever during those riots, Judge Widney plunged into the crowd, at the risk of his own life. Judge Widney held his gun high and fired a single shot. The crowd stepped back. And the future founder and first chair of USC then escorted a number of Chinese immigrants to safety.

It was at that moment, on that evening that the DNA of USC as a global institution was called into being. In that moment, on that evening, the ethos, the character, of USC began to take shape.

Character is destiny, and USC would have a global character. A few years later, Japanese students would be among USC's first graduates. And USC would develop the largest body of international alumni in the world, mostly from the emerging nations of the Pacific. USC would develop an international curriculum that benefits both our American and international students. USC would pioneer transcultural scholarship that addresses the pressing needs of this age.

What USC has accomplished locally and regionally can now be done at a global level.

The New City of Troy

While USC imitates no one, I do believe USC has the chance to serve as an intellectual engine in this century, in much the way Oxford University emerged earlier as the intellectual engine of the British Empire and commonwealth nations.

As our world today is shifting away from an Atlantic to a Pacific Century, USC is better positioned than anyone else to lead this change. To become the intellectual and cultural and spiritual fabric of a world that is tied to the Age of the Pacific. To become the foremost laboratory of experimentation of "East-West" ideas, in scholarship and the arts and media and journalism and culture. To become the campus where the influencers of the Pacific Age will be educated, shaped, and molded.

This is our moment. And, I believe, that should be our vision!

Do you know what alma mater *means? It means, literally, "Mother who feeds us all." Consider what it could mean for USC to firmly take its role as alma mater for this Age of the Pacific.*

Let the best young minds from across the Pacific Rim compete to receive a USC education. Let us build special scholarship programs for students represented from all Pacific Rim nations. Let them take full advantage of a highly diverse environment they won't find anywhere else.

Great talent exists in America and around the Pacific Rim. Let that talent be refined in the unique intellectual crucible here, which represents a dynamic blend of the arts and humanities and culture, and cutting-edge science and technology, and social sciences and professions.

Indeed, USC, as an American university, is strategically positioned to serve as the intellectual crucible—the intellectual melting pot—of the Pacific Rim.

Destiny has dealt a favorable hand to USC. Let us play this out wisely.

The hero Aeneas and the Trojans completed a great adventure that led to a new City of Troy, which would grow into mighty Rome. For the Trojans of USC and for Southern California, our own New City of Troy can indeed be a New Rome in Higher Education for the Age of the Pacific.

It was said, "A thousand roads all lead to Rome." And in the coming years all roads will lead to Southern California and a great university that sits at its center.

Does all this sound far too audacious? Does all this sound far too bold to be our goal?

Many prestigious universities attract brilliant people. But consider for a moment the full power, the full potential of our university: USC will allow brilliant people to make a dramatic difference, to improve the lives of women and men and children around our world!

And as we move forward in our new Great Journey, what are the signposts that we are approaching our destination?

When people around the world think of the intellectual giants of the 21st century, they will be thinking of the faculty and students of the University of Southern California.

When people look back in the next century at how the medical revolution exploded forth in life-giving ways, they will see that USC's stamp was placed upon that revolution, as well as on many other revolutions of the mind such as the arts and social sciences.

The critical mass of academic excellence on our two campuses will give us the academic gravitas necessary to pull everything else into USC's orbit.

We will see a dramatic boost in our ability to recruit the world's best graduate and Ph.D. students, who serve as the manpower and womanpower of America's research innovation enterprise.

We will celebrate a Trojan heritage of student athletics that will be more glorious than before. Yes, our Trojan student-athletes are indeed students first and foremost. And so our athletic heritage will demonstrate that the triumphs of athletics and the triumphs of education are the same, at their core. Body and mind, working together, in pursuit of excellence.

We will also know we are reaching our destination when the Trojans are known as the premier network of leaders across the Pacific Rim.

We will all enjoy access to the greatest international network of rain-makers and decision-makers—leaders in scholarship and business and government and the arts and culture.

Thanks to the dedication of countless Trojans and USC friends, USC has already made a remarkable impact.

But as we look ahead, and see what remains to be done, I would like to ask: Are we, the Trojan Family, ready to embark for the most important leg of this journey?

After all, the last part of the journey is often the most complex and the most costly and the most difficult. And yet the greatest prize of all lies ahead.

Let me draw your eyes to the familiar statue behind you, in the southwest corner of this park. Behold there is the figure of Tommy Trojan, who has stood guard for 80 years… without losing his youth or his strength or his optimism.

On the southwest-facing base of the statue are some words from Virgil's Aeneid. *I ask you to pass by the statue today and read those words, which are written in both Latin and English. You may need your glasses to read these lines, which are inscribed in very small letters: "Here are provided seats of meditative joy… where shall rise again the destined reign of Troy."*

Consider those words: "There shall rise again the destined reign of Troy." Those words call us to work together to claim destiny's promises, and to renew those promises within our individual lives and our collective lives. The destined reign of Troy is an intellectual community that has achieved undisputed elite status—at the very epicenter of global influence. When you are there, there is no doubt, there is no argument, you belong within the pantheon of world-class universities. There is no question that your voice shall be heard, and that your ideas are received. And there is no limit on the impact USC is able to make upon the world.

Ours will indeed be the task of nurturing and guiding this global, Pacific age, and rejuvenating the American pioneering spirit. Ours will be the privilege of finding new ways to bring healing to the ill and insight to the innocent. Ours will be a movement that illustrates the power of a diverse and democratic community in full blossom. Ours will be the task of shaping the most pressing debates of the day. Ours will be an ongoing rebellion against the conventional order of things, as we help individuals and societies, to consider and to create limitless possibilities for themselves.

So too ours will be an intellectual renewal which delights in uncovering and discovering new knowledge, so that we are tantalized by the chance that what we discover today will change what we believed yesterday.

All this is the Great Adventure. All this is the Great Journey. All this is the way forward to the Destined Reign of Troy.

Thank you, and Fight On, Always!

USC Village

Chapter 2

Fas Regna Trojae

The Campaign for the University of Southern California

Within the well-manicured, orderly, ivy-covered walls of higher education, caution and prudence are among the highest values. Universities, after all, are supposed to last for decades or centuries longer than businesses, and that explains their latent conservatism. USC and its Trojan Family have since their earliest days brought a blend of brashness, ambition, and entrepreneurialism that is unusual within the academy. These qualities powered the young university's ability to find supporters and partners as it grew rapidly.

No modern university rises to ultimate heights on its wits alone. Academic excellence, in our increasingly technical age, requires financial support from broad communities of people. As President Nikias put it, "The vision of our academic community outstripped our ability to pay for it." Therefore, USC's continuing dramatic progress would require rapidly increasing the level of philanthropic support it received—from alumni, parents, friends, corporations, and foundations alike.

As a result, USC embarked in 2011 on a historic, $6 billion fundraising campaign titled *Fas Regna Trojae* (or "the Destined Reign of Troy"). The campaign still has years to go, but it has already shattered national records and drawn surprised reactions across the world of higher education. It also continues a powerful pattern established decades earlier—what Nikias described as a "determination by each new generation of the Trojan Family to raise the bar for success much higher than before…and to leave behind a better university for the next generation."

USC's fundraising prowess reflects the same distinct marriage of strong ambition and noble purpose that first moved its founders to make a bet on an unlikely setting for a great university. As Edward P. Roski Jr., a longtime trustee and former chair of the board, explained in *Trojan Family Magazine*, "If you want to be in the elite, it takes investment." And the USC community

USC's rapid academic ascent was made possible by the collective efforts of more than 290,000 individual donors—some longtime members of the Trojan Family, others who are less directly connected to the university. At the 2014 groundbreaking for USC Village, President Nikias thanks donors and community residents who made the massive project possible.

Transformational Gifts: 2010–2015

The Campaign for the University of Southern California

Fas Regna Trojae, *the Campaign for the University of Southern California, was launched in 2010. The $6 billion goal was the largest ever in higher education at the time of its announcement. Buoyed by a number of transformational gifts, as well as contributions of every size from 290,000 individual donors, USC reached the $4.5 billion mark within five years.*

Anonymous Donor
$360 million to various university programs

David and Dana Dornsife
$200 million to name the USC Dornsife College of Letters, Arts and Sciences

W. M. Keck Foundation
$150 million to name Keck Medicine of USC

John and Julie Mork
$110 million for undergraduate student scholarships

Annenberg Foundation
$50 million for Wallis Annenberg Hall; and $15 million for student scholarships

Mark and Mary Stevens
$50 million to name the USC Mark and Mary Stevens Neuroimaging and Informatics Institute; and $20 million for Trojan athletics

Andre Young and Jimmy Iovine
$70 million to establish the USC Jimmy Iovine and Andre Young Academy for Arts, Technology and the Business of Innovation

Ming and Eva Hsieh
$50 million for the USC Ming Hsieh Institute for Research on Engineering-Medicine for Cancer

Glorya Kaufman
Historic gift to establish the USC Glorya Kaufman School of Dance

Price Family Charitable Fund
$50 million to name the USC Sol Price School of Public Policy

Gary K. and Alya Michelson
$50 million to create the USC Michelson Center for Convergent Bioscience

was determined to be nothing less than elite in carrying out its missions in teaching, research, patient care, athletic competition, and public service.

If many for-profit enterprises can be characterized by a competitive streak and a desire to be market leaders, and nonprofit enterprises by a desire to serve and benefit society, then USC's Trojan Family seems to be characterized by a competitive instinct to be the very best at the business of benefiting society.

A Short Financial History of the Trojan Family

Historically, the most established, productive, and influential research universities have been those with the benefit of vast monetary reserves, in the form of founding endowments, gifts, and other sources. Those reserves are essential to building and maintaining the highest level of academic quality. USC did not enjoy those advantages, and its leaders would have to be nimble in finding alternative pathways to excellence.

Judge Robert Maclay Widney and the school's other early boosters seemingly moved heaven and earth to create the humble, two-story college in 1880. Unlike many other universities, USC did not have billionaire industrialist founders or a state government willing to pay any expense to speed along academic growth. From its first days, it was forced by necessity to be financially savvy and restrained. That may have lowered its academic ceiling somewhat in early decades; but it also disciplined the university to move in wise and entrepreneurial ways in later years—especially as it began, more than half a century ago, to build its financial strength.

During the 1960s, USC underwent a radical transformation. It had long been an admired and beloved regional university that produced the key first waves of Southern California's professional class—the teachers, doctors, lawyers, entrepreneurs, artists, and others who fueled the region's growth. But this role was increasingly being shared with the dozens of other colleges and universities proliferating across the landscape. USC's role needed to change, or the venerable anchoring institution of Southern California would inevitably be less relevant to the region's future.

In fact, USC had ambitions to become a national academic player. To evolve into a strong research university, capable of competing nationally

for prestigious faculty, quality students, and research funding, it needed a focused plan.

Central to this process was the first major capital campaign in its history: the Master Plan for Enterprise and Excellence in Education, launched in 1961 by President Norman H. Topping in an effort to raise $106.7 million. Skeptics said USC was aiming too high, but it raced to that goal, and past it, in just five years. Topping had sought nothing less than a transformation of the university, and the success of the Master Plan fueled it. The campaign didn't simply make him a game-changing president in his own time; it also set a benchmark of lofty ambitions for each subsequent fundraising drive.

Topping's successor, John R. Hubbard, led the Toward Century II campaign, to prepare USC for its 1980 centennial. The effort netted $309.3 million in five years, tripling the previous campaign's total. Next, President James H. Zumberge's Leadership for the 21st Century campaign raised $641.6 million in six years, doubling the earlier record.

President Steven B. Sample announced the Building on Excellence campaign in the early 1990s. By the time that drive concluded in 2002, USC had raised $2.85 billion and earned a reputation as a force in the worlds of philanthropy and higher education.

Celebrating the launch in 2011 of the most ambitious fundraising campaign in the history of higher education (clockwise from top left): USC trustee and developer Rick Caruso; the official campaign pin, inscribed with the Latin phrase *fas regna Trojae* (the destined reign of Troy); university CFO Robert Abeles with Trustee John Mork.

The Longest Odds

The Trojan community in 2010 was determined to maintain its recent momentum. Yet economic headwinds had gained immense force by then. For all the successes of past decades, it seemed that USC—and universities everywhere, frankly—would need to dial down ambitions to more plausible levels. Every sector of society was moving from irrational exuberance to a more reasonable, cautious level of expectation. For USC, the tradition of successfully raising the bar for each subsequent capital campaign seemed overly ambitious under the circumstances.

When Nikias took office as USC's 11th president, the Dow Jones Industrial Average languished at about 10,000 points, higher than its March 2009 nadir of 6,547 but far below the recent record high of 14,165 in July 2007. Economists at the time debated whether the national and global economies were in recovery or stagnation. And even if the term "recovery" was used charitably, it was a jobless recovery, meaning that consumer sentiment (and presumably philanthropic generosity) would be muted.

"Trillions of dollars of wealth had evaporated," Nikias later said, "and no one was counting on that money ever being available again. Confidence was very low, and we knew it was the least promising environment possible in which to begin a fundraising campaign."

Yet USC leaders recognized that by moving forward aggressively at a time when many elite universities were retrenching, the Trojans could make, in Nikias's words, "a decade's worth of academic progress in just a few years." And such quick progress would be instrumental in helping the institution reach its loftiest goals.

So if reasonable observers expected USC to take a more modest approach than its usual habit of doubling the dollar goal of its previous campaign, they would be confounded. At the campaign launch event on September 15, 2011, Nikias announced an unprecedented $6 billion goal—six times higher than the original target of the previous campaign, and the highest ever publicly announced by any university.

The campaign had been dubbed *Fas Regna Trojae* (the Destined Reign of Troy), as a tangible expression of the drive to build a mighty new Troy in the spirit of Virgil's *Aeneid*.

The Nikias family (center) greets USC supporters at a reception preceding the September 2011 kickoff of the university's $6 billion fundraising campaign. Many higher education experts and observers were surprised by the size and scope of the campaign, due to the ongoing uncertainty in the global economy.

The Chronicle of Philanthropy, reporting the news, quoted experts who felt USC had bitten off a financial goal it would prove unable to chew. An article titled "Can USC Really Raise $6 Billion?" began ominously:

> Some fundraising experts are questioning whether the University of Southern California can really reach its audacious goal of raising $6 billion by 2018. No private organization has ever tried to collect that much from a single drive.
>
> The observers, who all wish to remain anonymous, said they want to see the campaign succeed, because in the sputtering economy, "the last thing we need is for a big capital campaign not to be successful," according to one seasoned fundraiser. If the high-profile campaign does not achieve its goals, he said, it could undermine donors' confidence in the viability of large nonprofit institutions and their ability to generate support.

The philanthropic and academic worlds soon found they could collectively exhale in relief. Far from reducing confidence in the ability of great institutions to aim high, USC's immediate success in the *Fas Regna Trojae* campaign boosted confidence across academia and set a new standard for top universities everywhere. Just months after USC's announcement, Stanford extended its own campaign in order to reach the $6.2 billion mark; and two years later, Harvard set a goal of $6.5 billion.

The announcement of the *Fas Regna Trojae* campaign's unprecedented $6 billion goal was like a shot heard around the world of higher education. Celebrating with 200 supporters in front of the Widney Alumni House are, from left to right: Senior Vice President Albert R. Checcio and his wife, Sue; Alumni Association president Lisa Barkett and her husband, Bill; First Lady Niki C. Nikias and President Nikias; and then-Board Chair Edward Roski and his wife, Gayle.

A Strategy for Success

How did the campaign succeed in its early phases beyond any reasonable prediction? Far more than being the recipient of good fortune, the USC community worked skillfully and strategically to create the best environment for success. Just as the university had made dramatic strides in improving the reputation of its student body and the influence of its faculty, it followed a coordinated path to shaping, articulating, and reaching for its fundraising goals. Nine strategies were involved.

1. An honest assessment of USC's capabilities

During the final years of the Sample presidency, Nikias, who was at that time provost, oversaw an analysis of how the university would need to develop and reorganize its fundraising infrastructure for the coming years. The school's

leaders hired the consulting group Grenzebach Glier and Associates to compare its fundraising operation with that of its peer universities, especially those that were currently conducting campaigns. It soon became clear that USC's relatively lean and decentralized operation would need to be overhauled and augmented before any campaign could begin. At the same time, the university defined clear priorities for where additional endowments and investments were required and where its academic foundation needed strengthening.

2. Recognition of the need for urgency

The economy's worrying vital signs suggested that any university seeking to raise money should have modest expectations at best. Many other schools

At an event celebrating the $70 million gift that established the USC Jimmy Iovine and Andre Young Academy for Arts, Technology and the Business of Innovation in 2013 are its founders, music industry icons Jimmy Iovine and Andre "Dr. Dre" Young; USC Roski dean Erica Muhl (the inaugural director of the academy); and President Nikias.

The Trojan Marching Band and dignitaries celebrate the naming of the USC Sol Price School of Public Policy in 2012. A $50 million gift from the Price Family Charitable Fund led to the formal renaming of the school in honor of the renowned entrepreneur, philanthropist, and USC alumnus.

deferred their fundraising campaigns. But USC's leadership believed a massive capital campaign of global scope would be the only way to fund the dreams that bound together the Trojan Family. This was indeed a challenge to an institution that prided itself on outperforming the expectations the outside world had for it.

Yes, the economic realities had created uncertainty; but as Nikias noted in many talks to the university community, "For a Trojan, what is uncertainty, after all, but the beginning of a great adventure?" For USC, the state of flux in higher education and the larger society promised a chance to do things in new ways, in order to move the university to the vanguard of progress.

Dana Dornsife, who (with her husband, David, a longtime trustee) would become the namesake of the USC Dornsife College of Letters, Arts and Sciences, captured the sense of urgency that moved the university's leadership. "USC is at a point where I think all of the stars are aligned," she told *Trojan Family Magazine*. "You only get those chances once in a while, and you better either move right then or you're going to miss your opportunity."

That belief renewed the university leadership's willingness to aim higher than others could have imagined. If USC operated like most institutions, raising its sights only after clear evidence of a sustained recovery, the window

of opportunity—the ability to make dramatic progress relative to its peers—would close, for a generation or more.

3. A clarion call that appealed to talented and successful people during uncertain times

At a time when everyone else was thinking small, USC was thinking big and acting accordingly. And this proved intoxicating to donors, potential faculty recruits, and many other constituencies.

Nikias's inaugural address, on October 15, 2010, had been broadly hailed as an inspiring and compelling charge for the Trojan Family to move faster—to

DANA AND DAVID
DORNSIFE
COLLEGE OF
LETTERS, ARTS
AND
SCIEN
UNIVERSITY OF SOUTHERN CALIFORNIA
1880
PALMAM QUI MERUIT FERAT

Trustee David Dornsife and his wife, Dana, made the largest gift in the university's history—$200 million—to name the USC Dana and David Dornsife College of Letters, Arts and Sciences in 2011. This both helped place the Trojans' daring fundraising campaign on sure footing and sent a message nationally about how USC had emerged as a premier place to invest in the future.

"run a marathon at a sprinter's speed," as the new president said, pledging to model such a pace personally.

Donors responded to Nikias's call to join the university community on the "journey of a lifetime." This was a rare chance to build something on a grand scale—at a time when others seemed content merely to survive. And it proved too much for many donors to resist. When some of the world's biggest banks were more inclined to sit cautiously on their cash piles than put them to the lending purposes for which they were accumulated, USC donors were willing to invest their fortunes in enduring forms of educational philanthropy.

And as it soon became clear, the president did not have to wait long to see others endorse the university's vision or put crucial resources behind it.

4. Expansion and centralization of USC's fundraising machine

When Albert R. Checcio took office as the senior vice president of university advancement in August 2010, USC employed a total of about 230 professionals for fundraising development, including staff in the Alumni Association. This staff was spread out across the institution's vast sweep of independent schools and research centers, operating in a mainly decentralized fashion.

Over the next four years, the university assembled a fundraising army 440 people strong, spanning every academic unit. Under Checcio's leadership, this team created and operated a fundraising machine appropriate for a campaign of the scope of *Fas Regna Trojae*. The development officers of all USC schools came together regularly to assess progress and plot strategy with the central development team.

The expansion of the fundraising staff required some careful pruning in other areas, especially given the fragile economy. All academic units were asked to trim their administrative expenses, in order to allow the university as a whole to maximize its ability to invest in long-term fundraising.

5. An immediate spring into action

It is one thing to brashly set a record-setting campaign goal; publicly announcing the goal is an even thornier matter. It is standard procedure for a university to avoid announcing a fundraising target until the campaign is well on its way to successful completion. Until that milestone, campaigns tend to run in a so-called quiet phase, to ensure that the goal will be reached without setbacks or readjustment downward. Universities typically test the philanthropic waters

Lisa Mazzocco joined USC in 2011 as its first chief investment officer. In that role, she oversees the investments made through the university's growing endowment, in order to maximize its financial and academic strength.

Senior Vice President Albert R. Checcio, architect of the overall USC *Fas Regna Trojae* campaign, tells attendees of the 2014 Widney Society Gala how their support is transforming the university's work in education, research, public service, and patient care.

by first trying to raise some 50 percent of their intended goal before making any public announcement. This is what Harvard did in late 2013, going public after first securing $2.8 billion in cash and pledges. In the case of Stanford, its $6.2 billion campaign involved a quiet phase that brought in $2.19 billion.

Thus, if USC intended to raise $6 billion, most observers in 2011 believed the university would be prudent not to make that goal public until a few years into the campaign.

Nikias and the trustees went against conventional wisdom and announced the $6 billion goal in the fall of 2011, with only the first one-sixth of the total amount—$1 billion in pledges—in hand. Nikias also stated that USC planned to reach that goal by 2018. This was seen as a risky move by many fundraising experts, who believed that the university didn't need to place a deadline on its dreams. The school's leadership did not make these announcements for the sake of being contrarian. They believed USC did not have the luxury of waiting too long before stating the goal (and therefore putting its reputation on the line), because they needed the Trojan community to move into full campaign mode immediately.

This approach also symbolized the difference between USC and the more staid higher education establishment. The measured strategy of other schools was indicative of their unwillingness to take risks or experiment. And USC's bold outlook captured the imagination of many around the nation.

6. Energizing the Trojan Family

To till the soil for the campaign, President and Mrs. Nikias hosted "Trojan Family Receptions" in key cities and regions across the United States. They met with alumni and supporters, connecting and discussing USC's progress and future potential; and they asked Trojans to consider the various ways they could advance the university's mission.

The president and first lady met with alumni across Southern California, including downtown Los Angeles, Orange County, Beverly Hills, San Diego, and Santa Barbara. To mobilize the Trojan Family at the national level, they

traveled to San Francisco, Sacramento, Chicago, New York, and Washington, D.C. All told, they reached nearly 4,000 members of the USC community in the early phases of the campaign.

Seasoned observers agree that the second half of a capital campaign is by far the most difficult, given that the most enthusiastic supporters have typically already made their most significant gifts. As the midpoint of the campaign approached, the Nikiases embarked on a second major tour, to keep supporters energized and focused on bringing the epic fundraising project to completion. Their itinerary included Phoenix, Chicago, San Francisco, Seattle,

Glorya Kaufman made a generous gift in 2012 to establish USC's sixth independent arts school—the USC Glorya Kaufman School of Dance. In 2014, the university breaks ground on the three-story facility that will house the school. From left: Founding USC Kaufman School dean Robert A. Cutietta, Glorya Kaufman, President Nikias, and USC Kaufman vice dean and director Jodie Gates.

Philanthropist and former USC athlete Fred Uytengsu attends the February 2014 grand opening of the Uytengsu Aquatics Center. The center was one part of a dramatic overhaul and improvement of facilities for the university's legendary athletics program.

Santa Monica, San Diego, Pasadena, Sacramento, Washington, D.C., Dallas, Boston, Houston, and Austin. This time they met with an even larger number of Trojans.

7. Bringing non-alumni into the life and work of USC

"To give away money is an easy matter and in any man's power," Aristotle said. "But to decide to whom to give it and how large and when, and for what purpose and how, is neither in every man's power nor an easy matter."

Most people give to causes or institutions with which they enjoy a particular long-standing connection. The "mythology" of USC is that its success in fundraising is fueled almost entirely by fanatically dedicated alumni.

However, the university's fundraising goes beyond those who are already part of the Trojan Family. A full 62 percent of dollars raised during the most recent years has come from non-alumni—including parents, friends, corporations, foundations, and other sources.

8. Paying more attention to donors of every giving level

For many years USC had been associated with a number of famous donors who gave transformational "mega-gifts" of eight or nine figures. University leaders now sought to create and celebrate a broader circle of contributors. One key aspect of this effort involved a long-term strategy to turn million-dollar

USC established the Widney Society in 2012 to recognize donors who have pledged or given more than $1 million to the university in their lifetime.

At the Widney Society's first annual gala, USC inducted more than 1,000 charter members into the society. Above, from left: Glorya Kaufman; Dana and David Dornsife; John Mork (USC's new board chair) and his wife, Julie; the president and first lady; and Pamela and Leonard Schaeffer.

donors into even greater supporters in the future. Donors who make generous, seven-figure gifts—and who feel that their gift is valued and put to good use—oftentimes give again at even higher levels.

The priority to focus a spotlight on donors who gave $1 million or more resulted in the creation of the USC Widney Society in November 2012. At a gala held adjacent to the venerable Widney Alumni House, President Nikias inducted some 1,282 charter members into the society—more than 300 of whom attended in person. This honor would forever associate their names with the name and legacy of the school's founder, who had shown unlimited energy and determination in his efforts to build a great university. Nikias praised the society members for following in Widney's footsteps and helping build a better USC that came ever closer to achieving its founder's first audacious vision for the university. The Widney Society continues to add hundreds of members annually, thanks to the success of the campaign. By 2015, it was 1,622 strong and growing.

9. Capitalizing on early momentum from trustees and other key figures

Support from the trustees was crucial to the campaign's progress. Trustees are the closest thing a great university has to real "owners." They in fact own and govern the university, in trust, for a season of its life. In actual practice, the

privilege of ownership requires modeling support for the institution in a way that invites others to join in.

Nikias deemed the participation of the trustees in the campaign "incredible." As of 2015, 80 trustees had given a total of $1.2 billion—a full quarter of the total raised. This indeed affirmed that USC's guardians and governors ardently put their money where their mission statement was.

The Marathon Begins—at a Sprinter's Pace

The dollar amount of the trustee support was not the only validation of the university's bold vision; the strategic timing of it was also meaningful.

President Nikias honors Trustee Ming Hsieh for his $50 million gift to revolutionize cancer research by bridging engineering, health, and medicine.

Trustee John Mork and his wife, Julie, pledged a $110 million gift to endow scholarships that would make a USC education accessible to talented students from any background. In April 2011, a bronze plaque honoring the Morks was added to a wall of honor in the Bovard Administration Building—a tradition started by Nikias to commemorate the university's most transformative donors. John and Julie Mork (center) are flanked by their son, Kyle Mork, and his wife, Kirsten (left), and their daughter, Alison Mork Hansen, and her husband, Brooks Hansen.

Trustees Wallis Annenberg and Ming Hsieh orchestrated their gifts so that the incoming president could announce them at the conclusion of his 2010 inaugural ceremony.

Annenberg, the head of the Annenberg Foundation, dedicated her $50 million gift to building a new home for the journalism school within the USC Annenberg School for Communication and Journalism. This facility would be a place where, amid all the promise and turmoil of the digital age, faculty and students would be equipped to pioneer cutting-edge approaches to delivering the information that is crucial to the soul and proper functioning of a democratic society.

Hsieh, a co-founder of Cogent, Inc., dedicated his $50 million gift to establish the Ming Hsieh Institute for Research on Engineering-Medicine for Cancer, which would generate creative sparks by combining the best engineering with the best medicine. In this way, it was an early endorsement of USC's plans to use interdisciplinarity to move ahead faster than the traditional leaders of higher education.

Shortly after the inaugural address, David and Dana Dornsife approached Nikias to discuss how they might be able to offer their own support of his vision in a manner that would reverberate and gain national attention.

At the inauguration ceremony, as master of ceremonies Dennis Cornell announced the incoming processional of deans, the Dornsifes had noticed that the College of Letters, Arts and Sciences—USC's largest and oldest academic unit—lacked a naming benefactor.

After discussions with Nikias and other administrators and trustees, in March 2011 the couple pledged a staggering $200 million to endow the College—the largest single gift in the university's history. Calling the school the "beating heart of this academic community," Nikias gratefully announced that the trustees had voted to rename it the USC Dana and David Dornsife College of Letters, Arts and Sciences.

David is a 1965 alumnus of the university, where he studied business and was a shot-putter on two national champion Trojan track teams. As chair

AUTOMATIC
CAUTION
DOOR

ABOVE: USC alumna and trustee Verna Dauterive celebrates the opening of Dr. Verna and Peter Dauterive Hall. The building was made possible by her $30 million gift to honor the memory of her late husband, Peter. With her at the September 2014 dedication ceremony are (left to right) President Nikias, then-Provost Elizabeth Garrett, and Trustee Leonard Schaeffer.

LEFT: USC cuts the ribbon on its state-of-the-art Wallis Annenberg Hall, a key addition to its Annenberg School for Communication and Journalism, in October 2014. From left: featured speaker Alex Witt, MSNBC anchor and USC alumna; President Nikias; Wallis Annenberg, the university's longest-serving trustee; and Annenberg School dean Ernest J. Wilson III.

of the Herrick Corporation, he heads the West Coast's largest steel fabricator. Dana is an executive in the field of architectural, electronic, interior, and lighting design. Together, they are Presidential Associates and key benefactors and advisers for the USC Brain and Creativity Institute.

Another mega-gift was soon in coming, to serve as a strategic investment in the new vision. Trustee John Mork and his wife, Julie, responded to Nikias's call to help make a Trojan education affordable to students from any walk of life. The cost of college was becoming a subject of national concern and debate. And Nikias had asserted that if a student was talented enough to attend USC, there should be no reason for that student to go anywhere else, no matter what the family's economic background was.

The Morks' solution was to offer $110 million to establish the Mork Family Scholars Program. The endowment would pay the tuition and living costs for selected undergraduates for a full four years.

Nine-figure gifts are exceedingly rare in higher education. Before Nikias took office, USC had received only five such gifts in its 130-year history. Now the university had brought in two donations at that level in just one semester. And a third, from the Keck Foundation, followed soon after, before the end of the first year of the campaign.

A key aspect of the vision Nikias had laid out for USC involved medicine. Given how the world's economic and cultural centers of gravity were tilting

from the Atlantic to the Pacific, he argued that the goal should be nothing less than to build the leading academic medical enterprise of the Pacific Rim. That goal seemed overly audacious to many; but in June 2011, the Keck Foundation gave its own metaphorical shot in the arm to the effort, pledging $150 million to bring USC's entire medical enterprise under the world-renowned Keck name.

The university proudly saluted its supporters publicly; but in some cases, they preferred anonymity. One donor pledged more than $350 million over the course of the campaign yet declined any public recognition. "I'd just like to remain a whale below the surface of the ocean," he told the president.

USC's unsurpassed intercollegiate athletic heritage had for generations inspired people around the country; and, as Nikias noted, it served as nothing

A number of donors stepped up in 2011 to allow USC to build the 110,000-square-foot John McKay Center and open its doors the following year. At the 2012 dedication (from left) are alumnus Scott Brittingham, Senior Associate Athletic Director J. K. McKay, Trustee Mark Stevens, then-Board Chair Edward P. Roski Jr., President Nikias, Trustee Ron Tutor, Athletic Director Pat Haden, and Senior Associate Athletic Director Mark Jackson.

Trustee and longtime supporter of Trojan athletics B. Wayne Hughes Sr. (center) stands beside a portrait honoring him in USC's John McKay Center, unveiled in 2012. With him are his son, B. Wayne Hughes Jr., and daughter, Trustee Tamara Hughes Gustavson.

less than the "glue that holds the worldwide Trojan Family together." This tradition demanded renewal and recommitment in the face of a number of internal and external challenges. Stepping up to this call to action, beginning in 2010 numerous donors made the athletics program the beneficiary of four years of unprecedented support, totaling a record $300 million.

As a result, USC broke ground on the $70 million, 110,000-square-foot John McKay Center in 2011 and opened its doors in just a year's time. The McKay Center provides a dramatic new home for the proud Trojan football program and for a variety of academic and athletic services for student-athletes. The school's leaders emphasized that it stood as a towering symbol of the institution's enduring aspirations to set the standard for the integration of both academic and athletic excellence at a great university. Donations also allowed for a $30 million renovation of the hallowed Heritage Hall and a $20 million transformation of the Uytengsu Aquatics Center, among other key facilities.

The rate of giving by a college's undergraduate alumni is a sign of loyalty tracked by many higher education observers. USC's alumni-giving participation rate, perhaps unsurprisingly, had always been a point of pride for the Trojans. In 2014, 41 percent of undergraduate alumni gave to their alma mater, representing a steady increase over the years. That number places it well ahead of leading public research universities, and even above private

WELCOME USC MARSHALL

The USC Marshall School of Business publicly launched its $400 million fundraising initiative with Hollywood flair, with a gala event at the Warner Bros. Studio in Burbank in May 2013. At left, President Nikias, Trustee Frank Fertitta, and USC Marshall School dean James G. Ellis begin the night on the red carpet. Above, Nikias greets Trustee Thomas Barrack at the event.

peer institutions such as Stanford, Penn, Northwestern, and Columbia.

Another striking sign of commitment by donors to USC's mission came in the form of the $1.26 billion given by parents of students. (Of course, with the university's long and cherished scion tradition, some overlap existed among trustees, alumni, and parents.) Still, the community saw something profound in the desire of so many parents—alumni or not—to give beyond the tuition price. It signaled that these parents weren't simply involved in a transaction that would help their child earn a diploma: They were believers in the deeper, broader, and more enduring mission of the university.

Midpoint Momentum

The early, well-publicized major gifts by trustees such as Wallis Annenberg, Ming Hsieh, David and Dana Dornsife, and John and Julie Mork helped create the momentum that USC needed in lieu of the extended quiet period that most universities employed. In turn, that momentum had catalyzed the campaign engine to bring in important gifts at many levels from the worldwide Trojan Family. Midway through 2015, USC was the beneficiary of:

- 4 donations of $100 million or more;
- 14 donations of $50 million or more;

- 27 donations of $25 million or more; and
- 115 donations of $5 million or more.

Once again, the university community felt its academic ambitions had been validated. More important than the hopeful feelings that the early successful fundraising engendered, the resources turbocharged progress in implementing USC's academic vision.

By early 2015, the Dow was at 18,000, far higher than the previous record prior to the recession. During the first moments of the recovery—while most observers had thought it prudent for universities to wait for greener economic pastures before embarking on major campaigns—USC had capitalized on the Trojan Family's commitment and its ability to engage new friends outside the school to make the most of the opportunity. By then it was undeniable that USC's gamble had paid off.

ABOVE, *clockwise from top left:* Donors making a difference: President Nikias visits Trustee B. Wayne Hughes Sr. on his Kentucky farm; Trustee Michele Dedeaux Engemann and her husband, Roger Engemann; and Nikias with Trustee Tamara Hughes Gustavson and her husband, Eric Gustavson.

RIGHT, *clockwise from top left:* President and First Lady Nikias with Trustee Andrew Viterbi and his wife, Erna; Trustee Ray Irani and Nikias; Trustee Daniel Epstein (right) with Viterbi School dean Yannis Yortsos; Trustee Ronald Tutor; President and First Lady Nikias with Board Chair John Mork and his wife, Julie; Nikias with surgeon Gary K. Michelson and his wife, Alya; and Trustee Jane Hoffman Popovich with her husband, J. Kristoffer Popovich.

Chapter 3

Mighty Pillars of a Growing University

The Students of USC

For generations, the USC student experience has been characterized by a global flavor, close and mutually supportive social connections, and the quintessential college spirit. In recent years, that experience has become sought after to a degree that impressed longtime observers and even the school's proudest alumni.

Word was getting out that USC offered a rare, perhaps unique environment for students in every field to grow, both intellectually and socially. What characterizes that environment? President Nikias said that it involves a "big college's resources with a small college's feel." It includes freewheeling intellectual exchanges between people in the sciences and technology, arts and humanities, and social sciences and professions. And it encompasses an immersive experience in the heart of Los Angeles, one of the most dynamic and forward-looking global cities anywhere. These qualities have made a seat at USC an increasingly prized commodity, first at the undergraduate level and later in the graduate realm.

Over the past few years, the university has made strategic investments in programs and facilities to enhance that rich learning environment, and the competition has increased all the more. In 2010, USC was receiving about 35,000 applications for the 2,700 places in its freshman class. By 2015, that number had passed 53,000—more than any other private research university.

Developing the Hybrid University

USC has focused on building an undergraduate student body that is not only intellectually gifted and motivated to succeed but also uniquely broad in its academic interests. The explicit goal has been to create an intentionally hybrid university, rather than a specialized institution—and to capitalize on the energy that results from the various realms coming into meaningful contact in a manner beyond the reach of peer institutions.

By any measure, the university's student body has become one of the best and brightest in the nation. Unique to USC, however, is the interplay of promising young minds across many fields: in science and technology, the professions, social sciences and humanities, and the performing and creative arts.

On Move-In Day, the president and first lady welcome the newest Trojans and their families, at one point posing with students for "selfies," along with Board of Trustees chair John Mork (top left). Hundreds of USC parents help their children settle in to their new home in the walls of Troy, then bid fond—but somewhat temporary—farewells, as Trojan Family Weekend is only about two months away.

As one of the nation's largest private universities, USC is comparable in scale to many elite public research institutions. Yet for years, its freshman class had boasted higher average SAT scores than any premier public school—a fact that continually surprised many alumni from rival universities.

As time went on, the numbers told an even more compelling story, and by 2015 USC's 2,700 freshman also compared favorably with their counterparts at renowned private peer institutions. Consider some relative perspective: Caltech's freshman class featured about 200 students of a rare, almost-perfect academic caliber (as defined by SAT and grade point average); yet USC's incoming class boasted three times that number—an astounding collection of talent in the sciences and technology. And while the Stanford freshman class of 1,700 students was often viewed as a benchmark of student quality, USC had just as many new undergraduates of that same quality (again, as defined by the shorthand of SAT scores and GPAs).

At the same time, in a sign of its academically diverse nature, USC was also home to another 1,000 students of the highest artistic merit—not as easily measurable by traditional scholarly statistics. In fact, USC had more top students in the creative and performing arts than many of the world's leading conservatories.

By 2015, a remarkable 6,000 USC students were enrolled in degree programs in the arts, attracted by its six world-class independent schools: the

PRINT | COPY | SCAN
V313w

USC Roski School of Art and Design, the USC School of Architecture, the USC School of Cinematic Arts, the USC School of Dramatic Arts, the USC Thornton School of Music, and the newly established USC Kaufman School of Dance. At these institutions, they could receive a best-of-class education in their chosen specialty while also enjoying the intellectual, cultural, and social benefits of a great research university.

The USC Undergraduate Experience

USC has continued to showcase its diversity in recent years as a selling point to attract the world's best students—not only in its broad commitment across many academic fields but also as the home to more international students than nearly any other American university. With its location in the heart of Southern California and its global heritage, USC could position itself as a dynamic and inviting place for the world's most ambitious young scholars.

It was increasingly clear to the university's leaders that the coming century would be more globally interconnected and would belong to those who could build productive connections, not only across academic disciplines but also between cultures and nationalities. And it was naturally evident that some regions would have a greater impact on emerging economic sectors than others.

The university's current student body hails from 128 nations, with exceptional representation from the areas likely to generate the most economic and cultural energy in coming decades—specifically the Pacific Rim and Latin America, including China, India, and Brazil. This diversity benefits both domestic and international students, enabling them to form relationships with peers from around the world who can later become their partners and creative collaborators in the new global village.

USC is also home to some 90 different formal religious views, as well as many informal ones. On campus, Jews, Muslims, Christians, Buddhists, and humanists come together to explore ideas, consider differences, and care for one another. The Office of the Provost pointed this broad community toward a vision that married the search for meaning with USC's core, uncompromisable priorities regarding intellectual freedom. Varun Soni, USC's dean of religious life and the first Hindu to hold such a position at an American university, shepherds an ecumenical army of chaplains who both minister to their individual flocks and connect them to the larger academic community.

USC's annual New Student Convocation in Alumni Park: They come from all 50 states and 115 nations, but they leave as Trojans for life, bound across continents and generations. In the first year of his presidency, Nikias expanded the ceremony significantly to create a more dramatic rite of passage for incoming students and their parents.

A Great University Cannot Be Franchised

A central belief guiding the university's leaders was that its future lay in building the best learning environment possible on its Los Angeles campuses—rather than in franchising the USC experience through either foreign satellite campuses or online undergraduate programs. This placed USC in contrast with some of its peers. New York University, for example, was aggressively developing campuses in the Middle East and Asia, while Stanford and MIT were working on free, massive open online courses (MOOCs) to make their undergraduate offerings available worldwide.

Varun Soni, dean of religious life, is the first Hindu to serve in such a role at an American university. He chaplains a global student community representing more than 90 religious views.

President Nikias has been an ardent and unapologetic champion of the culture that exists on a great university campus. "There is a reason that American research universities have remained the envy of the world and a magnet drawing the world's best minds," he said. "There is a unique environment in these universities and a set of nonnegotiable principles: a commitment to freedom of academic inquiry and expression, gender equality, entrepreneurialism and shrewd risk-taking, the relentless search for truth, to diversity and even to old-fashioned school spirit. A hamburger may taste the same in Boston or Bahrain, but a great university experience like the one at USC cannot be franchised elsewhere. Instead, we must protect it and refine it on our own campus."

Administrators and faculty viewed the ever-rising popularity of USC as a boon—but also as an obligation. "If we're bringing in the best students in every kind of field from around the world," Nikias told alumni supporters, "then we owe it to them to give them the best learning experience possible—a singular kind of experience they can't get elsewhere. We need to find the resources to make this happen."

One key step in building that environment involved becoming a truly residential university. Despite USC's renown for school spirit, just a generation

Author Pico Iyer offers the keynote address at USC's 2015 Baccalaureate Ceremony. The multi-faith celebration, held annually in Bovard Auditorium on the eve of commencement exercises, has in recent years drawn a slate of renowned speakers, including actor and humanitarian Rainn Wilson and journalists Lisa Ling and Krista Tippett.

earlier it served as a commuter college for the majority of its students. A succession of administrations understood that the university's commitment to quality would require creating an atmosphere in which undergraduates, graduates, and faculty could all play active roles in a totally immersive academic community. With each passing decade, facilities had been added as steps toward that goal.

Over the past five years, USC has finally established itself as a genuinely residential university, with what Nikias called a "24/7 learning and living environment, both inside and outside the classroom." All campus dormitories have been reconfigured as residential colleges, complete with faculty masters and a slate of regularly planned academic and cultural activities. The experience is closer to the classic European college model, while simultaneously tapping

into the full cultural offerings of Southern California.

The groundbreaking of USC Village in the fall of 2014 represented another major milestone. When complete, this housing and retail development will serve as the communal center of the academic and local community. It will also include the USC Kathleen L. McCarthy Honors College, which will house some 600 of the university's most talented undergraduates.

Recruiting the Best and Brightest Across All Boundaries

With the increasing power of the USC brand, student interest in the university has continued to rise. Both the caliber and the diversity of the freshman class have grown incrementally each year, despite the challenge of making annual

In 2014, work begins on the $650 million USC Village, north of the University Park Campus, slated for completion in 2017. Representing the largest development project in the history of South Los Angeles, USC Village will add 2,700 student beds and complete USC's generation-long transformation from commuter school to first-rate residential university.

The "V for Victory" salute binds all members of the Trojan Family, whether they are celebrating USC spirit on campus or encountering fellow alums in far-flung locations around the world.

progress in student quality at a school that was already highly selective. This trend was not serendipity but rather a coordinated and structured effort of the admissions staff.

In 2009, Nikias, who was then provost, worked with Katharine Harrington, who oversaw both undergraduate and graduate admissions and financial aid, to develop an undergraduate recruiting strategy that brought in the highest level of students while being simultaneously far-reaching and inclusive of many underserved communities.

The strategy was both national and global in scope. While the university traditionally brought in undergraduates from across the country, the leadership made a symbolic decision in 2010 to represent all 50 states in each freshman class, through more intentional recruiting in all regions.

"Before Provost Nikias asked us to dramatically extend our reach, we were visiting about 600 high schools a year, all in the U.S.," said Harrington. "But there are many more excellent high schools than that. And there are about 2,700 seats in the freshman class each year. We were given the resources we needed, and now we visit more than 2,200 schools in all 50 states, and in 15 other countries. This has made a tremendous difference in our ability to attract the best and brightest students from all over the United States and the world."

Mork Scholars arrive on Catalina Island (left) for a weekend-long retreat at the USC Wrigley Institute for Environmental Studies. Later in the weekend, President Nikias and Trustee John Mork hold an informal conversation with the Mork Scholars (above left). Mark Torres (right) is a PhD candidate in earth sciences and a recipient of the William M. Keck Foundation Graduate Endowed Fellowship. Stamps Scholar Eric Deng (bottom left) and Clay Shieh construct a robot for an academic competition.

"I offered Katharine up to 50 new staff positions to build the sort of recruitment force necessary for our strategy," Nikias said. "But she's been making it work with just 35. Katharine and her team have worked incredibly well along the way."

The student body also reflected a level of ethnic and socioeconomic diversity rare for a private university. Some 23 percent of the freshman class in 2015 was made up of underrepresented minorities. Among the nation's 35 leading private universities, USC ranked first in the enrollment of underrepresented minorities, in total numbers and percentage of the total student body (counting both undergraduate and graduate students). It also ranked first in the enrollment of Hispanic students, in both total numbers and percentage; and second in the enrollment of African-American students in total numbers.

As a national debate raged over whether the country's premier colleges were doing enough to create access for economically disadvantaged students, USC's efforts reflected the high priority the university placed on ensuring that talented young people from every walk of life could benefit from the unique experience and educational opportunities it had to offer.

Accordingly, its leaders focused on restructuring administrative processes to maximize money directed to student scholarships. This commitment resulted in an unrestricted financial-aid pool of $300 million from USC's own sources—the largest offered by any American university. And it represented a

A student in the USC Roski School of Art and Design meticulously brings a design to life. The university has boosted funding support for all of its top graduate students, in order to strengthen its position as a place where the most promising scholars of the next generation could achieve their full potential.

65 percent surge over the $180 million it had offered just five years earlier.

Another remarkable figure is that about one in seven incoming Trojans represented the first generation in his or her family to attend college. Approximately 23 percent were from lower-income families eligible for federal Pell Grant assistance. *The New York Times* reported that USC ranked third nationally among private institutions in Pell Grant enrollment, and first among those west of Chicago.

USC also stepped up its traditional practice of welcoming high-need transfer students who had proved their academic mettle at community colleges. In 2014, USC brought in 824 community-college transfer students, mostly from lower socioeconomic backgrounds, to complement its 18,000-strong undergraduate population. Tellingly, most of the university's private school peers did not accept such transfers.

President Nikias wrote a feature article in *The Washington Post* that fall, suggesting that USC's peers follow its lead and begin to accept transfers from community colleges, so that private universities as a group could help solve the college-access problem that vexed so many families, experts, and policy makers. Nikias pointed out that 91 percent of USC's community-college transfers went on to earn degrees, a figure roughly equal to the overall student population. This,

The new Wallis Annenberg Hall, opened in 2014, boasts a state-of-the-art newsroom, the Chen/Moonves and CBS Media Center, which quickly became the envy of both working professionals and peer schools of communications and journalism.

he argued, should negate any concerns that those students would diminish the effectiveness or brand of private school educations.

While students at some universities were graduating with high levels of debt, about half of USC undergraduates completed their education with no outstanding loans. Those who did take on debt left owing an average of $23,000, a very manageable figure by national standards. And while default rates of 10 percent or higher were not uncommon on student loans, the average figure at USC was less than 1.6 percent.

USC's strategy was proving successful in providing the resources to allow qualified students from all backgrounds to enter the university—and to minimize the number of graduates burdened with long-term educational debt. In the crucial area of making sure entering students become degree

USC has made it a priority to support and honor Trojans who serve in the American armed forces. At the 2012 Veterans Appreciation Dinner, Trustee William Schoen (left) dons a personalized USC bomber jacket presented to him by Colonel Alvah E. Ingersoll III of the USC Naval ROTC. Schoen and his wife, Sharon, have generously supported scholarships for veterans at the university.

recipients, USC has made steady progress, by increasing the amount of financial aid available to families in need, creating a stronger residential university experience, and improving student access to effective academic advisement. In 2010, USC's graduation rate stood at 89 percent—an impressive rise from a few decades earlier, when it was a fairly ordinary 55 or 60 percent. And by 2015, that rate had risen to 92 percent, joining the rarefied heights of truly elite institutions.

Serving Those Who Serve the Nation

After World War II, the GI Bill made higher education and a better life available to millions of returning veterans, lifting the larger economy and society in the process. Faithful to that spirit, USC has taken special actions in recent years to open its doors to those committed to national service, and to support its military student population—which in 2015 numbered nearly 1,000 veterans and ROTC participants.

David Petraeus, retired four-star general and ex-CIA director, joined the university in 2013 as a Judge Widney Professor and took these students under his wing as an adviser. And Trustee Edward P. Roski Jr., both a former chair of the USC board and a former Marine, led the effort to establish an annual event honoring the students' service to the United States. The Veterans Appreciation Dinner has become one of the university's most cherished traditions.

Improving Graduate Education

As the USC undergraduate experience gained "buzz" nationally and internationally, the next opportunity—and imperative—was to strengthen the graduate programs across the university's 19 independent schools and associated

Retired four-star general David Petraeus leads students on a morning run through the Los Angeles Memorial Coliseum. He joined the USC faculty as a Judge Widney Professor in 2013, with a particular focus on developing and mentoring ROTC students.

academic research centers. USC was actively cultivating a reputation as a place where the top scholars of tomorrow—the very best graduate, doctoral, and postdoctoral students—congregated. This reputation was crucial to attracting the funding and support necessary for USC's signature research initiatives.

Shortly after Nikias became provost in 2005, USC began allocating internal funding to new categories of exceptional graduate students, luring many away from other premier research universities. Later, under both Nikias and his successor as provost, Elizabeth Garrett, USC expanded its efforts to gain external support for PhD and postdoctoral students, as graduates with a track record of outside funding are more competitive in the job market and more likely to go on to shape the future of their respective disciplines.

These initiatives have shown clear results. The number of PhD students at USC with NSF Graduate Research Fellowships has grown dramatically, increasing more than tenfold in less than a decade, from three in 2007 to 32 in 2015. And in the 2015–2016 academic year alone, 73 USC doctoral students secured major nationally competitive awards, including:

- Seven National Institutes of Health National Research Service Award fellowships;
- Three Department of Defense National Defense Science and Engineering Graduate fellowships;

- Three Department of State Fulbright fellowships;
- Three Haynes Foundation fellowships; and
- Three NSF Dissertation Research Improvement Grants.

USC's PhD students also received fellowships from the Department of Energy, NASA, the Social Science Research Council, the Mellon Foundation, the Ford Foundation, and the American Association of University Women. As the year began to unfold, USC students were selected for a Google Dissertation Fellowship, a finalist spot in the Fannie and John Hertz Fellowship, and many other honors.

USC also significantly boosted its postdoctoral fellows program, increasing the number at the university and its affiliates to more than 600 by 2015. Additionally, the Graduate School at USC launched a PhD Achievement Award for those who demonstrated exceptional accomplishments during their Trojan careers, based on overall record, publications, job offers, and other honors. As of 2015, 21 students had received the award, representing the Dornsife College, Marshall School, Viterbi School, and Annenberg School, among others.

Reshaping the Online Education Revolution

By 2011, several leading universities had begun offering some of their courses free on the Internet, open to anyone who wanted to benefit from the expertise of elite faculty. These classes—known as "massive open online courses," or MOOCs, for short—were intended to make those schools' undergraduate offerings accessible to hundreds of millions around the world.

Waves of enthusiasm and excitement—as well as concern—swept the landscape of academia, media, and government. Had society finally found a low cost or even free way to educate its billions of young citizens? Would traditional university campuses become obsolete? Many experts even pronounced that 2013 would be "the year of the MOOC." The mad scramble was on to build a virtual university that could do what traditional schools seemingly could not. Smart institutions knew that they needed to take a leadership role in the technological vanguard, or risk being pushed aside.

USC's approach was contrarian, based on its distinct academic values. In a lengthy report to the university community in August 2012, Nikias pointed

USC graduation, a beloved family tradition since 1884, takes on a modern touch during the 132nd annual commencement ceremony in 2015. The university now confers some 15,000 degrees annually at the undergraduate, graduate, doctoral, and professional levels.

to some changes as inevitable but dismissed others as hype. Crucially, he announced that USC had decided not to develop online degree programs for undergraduates. This policy was rooted in a core belief that the best learning experience is inherently social at the undergraduate level. This meant that the university would continue to develop an unrivaled experience for students—characterized by the diversity and intellectual breadth of its student body, its array of cultural opportunities, and the establishment of a fully immersive, residential learning and living environment.

However, Nikias went on to say that *graduate* education was ripe for reinvention through the opportunities offered by online interaction. Here he credited the faculty with finding a path that wed classic, uncompromising

academic values with new technology. "Quietly and without fanfare," he wrote, USC's faculty had developed a "global online graduate education enterprise that features academic breadth and economic viability." The USC model, which focused on graduate as well as continuing and professional studies, made a first-rate education possible for people in 40 nations, Nikias wrote, "while maintaining the all-important standards of academic rigor, integrity, and quality."

This balance was far harder to accomplish than many experts in academia and the media had initially realized. By 2013, a considerable backlash against MOOCs was under way. Media reports noted that once one looked

After being pronounced "Trojans for life," prepared to navigate together the uncertainties and adventures before them, USC graduates celebrate the beginning of a new chapter.

past the hyperbole, it was clear that most online education programs had terrible academic outcomes and unsustainable business models.

Meanwhile, at USC, an impressive 8,700 tuition-paying students were enrolled in online graduate programs by 2015. Revenues had by then reached $150 million, an unprecedented figure for any traditional, nonprofit American university. USC's programs were life-changing for many. In one example, the spouse of a military service member interviewed for a university news outlet said she was grateful for the ability to pursue quality graduate education in social work, despite the prospect of frequent relocation.

A particularly notable offering was developed at USC's Rossier School of Education: Its lauded Master of Arts in Teaching online program now serves hundreds of students and professionals around the country. The MAT program, which received the 2011 International Award for Innovative Practices in Higher Education in Washington, D.C., successfully places some 90 percent of its graduates in meaningful employment positions or advanced study.

Nikias expressed pride that USC's online graduate students were becoming increasingly integrated into the overall university community. "Online and hybrid program students are creating their own USC student organizations," he wrote, "affiliating with on-campus organizations and even trying out for the Trojan Marching Band. And hundreds of online students and their families now proudly participate in our spring commencement ceremonies. They are becoming, in all respects, full and valued members of the Trojan Family."

The USC leaders believed that the university was in a position to build a distinct experience and brand that could not be replicated—in either the virtual world or the traditional one. In that sense, the Trojans were once again using disruption and uncertainty as their allies in realizing their destiny.

In Memoriam

USC graduate students Ming Qu and Ying Wu, both 23 and from China, were killed in Los Angeles in April 2012. In July 2014, Xinran Ji, a 24-year-old graduate student from China, was killed near campus. Both tragedies provoked international outpourings of grief and prayer. The events also spurred the USC community to enhance security measures on campus and in USC's surrounding urban Los Angeles neighborhoods.

A week and a half after the 2012 incident, President Nikias appeared at a gala dinner held by the Committee of 100 to accept its Advancement of U.S.-China Relations award on behalf of USC. In his remarks, the president spoke of an unwavering determination to work toward creating

the best possible living and learning environment for USC students from every state and nation.

"Death and life indeed have their determined appointments. Riches and honor indeed depend on the mercies of heaven," Nikias said, echoing the words of Confucius. "But we each—we all—have roles to play, to bring the best of heaven here today, for our families and our communities."

President Nikias reiterated that commitment in an address to members of the university community later that year, saying, "Adversity makes us stronger, more focused and more determined to achieve our noble goals."

LEFT AND ABOVE: President Nikias honors the late Ming Qu and Ying Wu at a massive memorial service held for the grieving Trojan Family at the Shrine Auditorium.

TOP: Xinran Ji, a graduate student at the USC Viterbi School of Engineering, lost his life in July 2014.

President Nikias offers his annual State of the University address in February 2015. In his remarks, Nikias discussed the USC faculty's distinct opportunities to provide a blueprint for a new manner of research university that addresses the needs and concerns of today's world.

Chapter 4

Solidifying a Foundation for Excellence

Building Up the Scholarly Faculty

On a cool day in December 2013, USC professor Arieh Warshel stepped forward in Stockholm's famed concert hall to receive the Nobel Prize in Chemistry from King Carl XVI Gustaf of Sweden. Seated nearby were President Nikias and First Lady Niki C. Nikias, who made the transatlantic trek to celebrate this milestone, not only for Warshel, but for the larger academic community.

Indeed, the rapid transformation of USC's faculty into a global intellectual force constituted perhaps the most remarkable aspect of the school's rise. It has been said, without much exaggeration, that the faculty of the university *is* the university. The reputation, influence, and productivity of an American research institution—including the ability to attract funding and top students (especially at the graduate level)—directly correlate to the level of confidence the larger world has in its professoriate.

In 2010, the faculty comprised a large and accomplished body of experts, teachers, and discoverers spanning 19 schools and scores of disciplines. However, an academic ceiling was hovering overhead that limited the university's ability to gain the outside support and attention necessary to be at the vanguard of progress in multiple key fields.

For instance, USC aspired to compete against schools such as Columbia University. Although the latter is a much smaller institution, it had twice as many members of elite national academies on its faculty and eight Nobel laureates, while USC had just one. There was no way around it: Although the university had an excellent existing teaching body, it did not have enough "superstars" to compete against its peers nationally and achieve its ambitious research goals.

The academic leadership made it a high priority to remedy this situation—and to do so while a small window of opportunity remained temporarily open. The economic downturn had placed many universities under intense fiscal

OF SOUTHERN
1880
CALIFORNIA

pressure, even those with vast endowments. USC, by contrast, was financially stable and nimble enough to convince some of the world's most outstanding experts that, going forward, it could provide the setting where they could best realize their ambitions.

For all the importance of the faculty within American universities, support for their role among the public, the media, and elected officials has somewhat diminished in recent decades. Many argued that more efficient ways than the entrenched bureaucracy of the tenured professoriate must exist, and that new models would soon replace the traditional one.

In his first address to the Trojan teaching staff, in early 2011, Nikias took a decidedly opposing view. He spoke of the timeless academic values that guided universities such as theirs, and pointed to the faculty as the chief stewards of those uncompromisable core principles. He also spoke as one with an enduring bond with his colleagues, having been one of their peers for two decades.

Nikias praised the tenured professoriate for vigilantly "standing sentinel" over the principles and mission of the university, while commending those faculty outside the traditional tenure track for adding energy and fresh perspective to the scholarly pursuit. "Not an hour of the day slips by without my remembering that the faculty are the foundation of a university," Nikias said. "The scholarly faculty are the foundation of all academic excellence, and the cornerstone of all of a university's aspirations." He then went on to discuss an aggressive, double-pronged strategy to strengthen USC's "academic foundation."

First, the university would dramatically step up its efforts to support its current scholars. This involved an escalation of campaigns to procure external research funding (the lifeblood of American research universities) and increased attention on promoting their work for outside honors and awards, which would lead to more recognition for the university as a whole. It also entailed the creation of centralized incentives for researchers from different USC schools to collaborate innovatively, in a manner that did not come easy to their peers at other institutions.

Second, USC would work to attract new scholars who could partner creatively with current ones and turbocharge the overall level of productivity

Elizabeth Garrett, an accomplished legal scholar and academic leader, was installed as USC's first female provost in February 2011. After gaining national attention for her work as the school's second-ranking officer, she was named the first female president of Cornell University in September 2014.

on campus. These would be difference-makers and game changers—women and men who could bring both funding and academic gravitas with them and drive progress in more than one field. These "better-than-excellent faculty," Nikias later said, "could bring everything into orbit for USC academically, if they were recruited strategically and placed in the proper roles of leadership."

In some ways these tactics mirrored the manner in which USC had rapidly built one of the nation's most selective undergraduate student bodies some years earlier; careful recruitment of top prospects increased USC's profile and raised everyone's game, fostering the best forms of competition and collaboration. Engaging star faculty, of course, is a more elaborate and expensive process. And given how universities function, bringing radical change within the professoriate can be like trying to get an aircraft carrier to maneuver with the agility of a speedboat.

However, as was often proven to be the case at USC, the 2008 recession provided opportunities for those who were willing to look for them. The trustees and senior leadership realized that many of the world's best scholars were feeling constrained at other elite universities, both public and private,

Longtime USC professor Michael Quick took office as the university's provost in April 2015. Quick, a neuroscientist who has won numerous honors for teaching and research, previously served as executive vice provost to Elizabeth Garrett.

which had scaled down expectations and funding for their faculty due to the economic crisis. Some of these individuals would be drawn by the opportunity to be involved with a university that still spoke of high goals and pledged strong support for their work.

In the early going of the process, Nikias likened it to a stealth project, with no formal public announcement. "We can announce each superstar as she arrives," he told his colleagues, "but otherwise we must work quietly." That strategy would allow USC to identify the best prospects and recruit them with minimal resistance or competition.

The university leadership targeted game changers across all fields: in medicine, the sciences, and engineering, of course; but also in the humanities (history, philosophy, and classics); the social sciences (including economics and business); and the arts, communication, and media.

Nikias believed that such a faculty initiative had to be a joint venture of the offices of the president and the provost. The president would guide and push along the initiative, while the provost would coordinate the process of bringing in the talented new scholars, who in turn would dramatically increase the overall level of academic productivity. This would provide, he predicted, a "critical mass of academic excellence on our two campuses, which would generate much greater success over time than mere incremental improvement would."

When Nikias took office as president, Elizabeth Garrett was USC's acting provost, chief academic officer, and second-in-command. She had already served as Nikias's trusted chief lieutenant during his previous five years as provost, gaining progressively more oversight in the areas of academic planning and the university budget. Following a national search that examined scores of potential candidates, an advisory committee unanimously recommended Garrett to assume the office on a permanent basis. She was formally installed as USC's first female provost on January 11, 2011.

When Garrett took office, USC's professoriate boasted fewer than 40 National Academy members. Within four years, that number had risen dramatically, to 66. This gain came from both promotion of the work of current scholars and aggressive efforts to bring in additional superstar talent from institutions with global profiles for research excellence, including Harvard, Caltech, Stanford, Michigan, Northwestern, the Cleveland Clinic, UCLA, and Scripps.

Among the academic trailblazers on the USC faculty are (clockwise from top left): Andrew P. McMahon, director of the Eli and Edythe Broad Center for Regenerative Medicine and Stem Cell Research at USC; Stephen Gruber, director of the USC Norris Comprehensive Cancer Center; and Mark Humayun, co-director of the USC Roski Eye Institute.

USC's academic leaders believed that the acquisition of such talent signaled internationally that it was the destination where the world's most ambitious people could do their best work.

A Chance to Reach Higher: New Scholars in Science, Medicine, and Technology

Fittingly, some of the first and most newsworthy of USC's recruitments were in medicine, biology, and health-related fields. Beginning in 2010, USC announced an array of hires in these key areas, and by 2015 it had brought in hundreds of new faculty, clinicians, and researchers to the Keck School of Medicine alone. Significantly, many of these accomplished professionals spanned several departments and were viewed as catalysts for breakthroughs at the intersections and boundaries of different disciplines.

In 2011, acclaimed researcher Stephen Gruber became one of the university's first prominent recruitments in the sciences. He came from the University of Michigan to serve as the director of the USC Norris Comprehensive Cancer Center. Gruber was a master of clinical translational medicine, an area of growing significance in which USC was positioned to excel.

The following year, Andrew P. McMahon arrived from Harvard University. He took on the directorship of the Eli and Edythe Broad Center for Regenerative Medicine and Stem Cell Research at the Keck School of Medicine of USC and became chair of the department of stem-cell biology and regenerative medicine.

When McMahon became open to the idea of leaving Harvard, USC was not the front-runner for his next destination. As he told *The Chronicle of Higher Education:*

> Honestly, USC was the dark horse. I had more friends at UCSF, and I knew the institution better. And, of course, Harvard is a great place. But I became more convinced about the potential of USC through talking to the president, the provost, and the dean of the medical school. Stem-cell biology is at a tipping point where all sorts of new science is going to emerge. People are thinking about practical applications. That's been a strength of Harvard's stem-cell institute. And USC is strongly invested in moving research from bench to bedside.

That same year, USC reached across the Southern California region to recruit two new deans.

In April 2012, Pinchas Cohen, the former vice chair for research at the UCLA School of Medicine, was named the dean of the USC Davis School of Gerontology. Cohen's expertise in human development and medical issues surrounding the aging process made him ideally suited to guide a field that is quickly growing in importance.

The following month, USC announced the hiring of Steve A. Kay as the dean of the Dornsife College of Letters, Arts and Sciences. Kay, a member of the National Academy of Sciences, had been the dean of biological sciences at UC San Diego and is widely regarded as one of the world's leading scholars in the study of genes and circadian rhythms.

These early key hires dramatically demonstrated USC's ability to recruit some of the world's best talent from other elite private and public research universities and its intention to be a pacesetter in the crucial frontiers of science and medicine. The new faculty embodied, in words and actions, the scope of USC's academic ambitions.

All the recruitments were also made with cross-campus collaboration in mind. The concept of interdisciplinarity had long been a priority within higher education; but in practice, turf battles, budgets, and egos often prevented true collaboration. At USC, the vast sweep of 19 professional schools and affiliated

Transformative Faculty Recruitments: Science, Medicine, and Technology

Paul Aisen, Director, USC Alzheimer's Therapeutic Research Institute (USC ATRI) in San Diego; Professor of Neurology, Keck School of Medicine

Salman Avestimehr, Associate Professor of Electrical Engineering Systems

Vadim Cherezov, Professor of Chemistry

Pinchas Cohen, William and Sylvia Kugel Dean's Chair in Gerontology, USC Davis School of Gerontology; Executive Director, Ethel Percy Andrus Gerontology Center

Peggy Farnham, Professor and W. M. Keck Chair in Biochemistry and Molecular Biology; Chair of the Department of Biochemistry and Molecular Biology

Valery Fokin, Professor of Chemistry

Scott E. Fraser, Elizabeth Garrett Chair in Convergent Bioscience; Provost Professor of Biological Sciences and Biomedical Engineering

Rick A. Friedman, Professor of Otolaryngology

Gerhard J. Fuchs, Professor of Clinical Urology; Executive Director, USC Institute of Urology (Beverly Hills)

Stephen B. Gruber, H. Leslie Hoffman and Elaine S. Hoffman Chair in Cancer Research; Professor of Medicine and Preventive Medicine, Keck School of Medicine; Director, USC Norris Comprehensive Cancer Center

W. Daniel Hillis, Judge Widney Professor of Engineering and Medicine

Jae U. Jung, Distinguished Professor of Molecular Microbiology and Immunology and Pharmacology and Pharmaceutical Sciences; Fletcher Jones Foundation Chair of Molecular Biology and Immunology; Hastings Foundation Professor of Molecular Microbiology and Immunology

Steve A. Kay, Anna H. Bing Dean's Chair, USC Dornsife College; Professor of Molecular and Computational Biology, Neurology, Physiology, and Biophysics

Peter Kuhn, Dean's Professor of Biological Sciences

Jay R. Lieberman, Professor of Orthopaedics and Biomedical Engineering; Chair of the Department of Orthopaedic Surgery

Andrew P. McMahon, W. M. Keck Provost Professor of Stem Cell Biology and Regenerative Medicine and Biological Sciences; Chair of the Department of Stem Cell Biology and Regenerative Medicine; Director, Eli and Edythe Broad Center for Regenerative Medicine and Stem Cell Research

Laura Mosqueda, Professor of Family Medicine and Geriatrics (Clinical Scholar); Chair of the Department of Family Medicine

John Niparko, Leon J. Tiber and David S. Alpert Chair in Medicine; Professor of Otolaryngology—Head and Neck Surgery; Chair of the Caruso Department of Otolaryngology—Head and Neck Surgery

Jong-Shi Pang, Epstein Family Chair; Professor of Industrial and Systems Engineering

Daniel Pelletier, Professor of Neurology; Eric and Peggy Lieber Chair in Neurology

Bradley Peterson, Professor of Pediatrics and Psychiatry

Oleg Prezhdo, Professor of Chemistry

Larissa Rodriguez, Professor of Urology; Associate Provost for Faculty and Student Initiatives in Health and STEM

Jonathan Samet, Distinguished Professor and Chair of Preventive Medicine; Flora L. Thornton Chair in Preventive Medicine; Director, USC Institute for Global Health

Raymond C. Stevens, Provost Professor of Biological Sciences and Chemistry

Paul M. Thompson, Director, Imaging Genetics Center; Associate Director, USC Mark and Mary Stevens Neuroimaging and Informatics Institute; Professor of Ophthalmology, Neurology, Psychiatry, Radiology, Pediatrics, and Biomedical Engineering

Arthur W. Toga, Director, USC Mark and Mary Stevens Neuroimaging and Informatics Institute; Provost Professor of Ophthalmology, Neurology, Psychiatry and Behavior Sciences, Radiology, and Biomedical Engineering

Rohit Varma, Grace and Emery Beardsley Chair in Ophthalmology; Chair of Ophthalmology; Professor of Ophthalmology and Preventive Medicine; Director, USC Roski Eye Institute

Berislav V. Zlokovic, Professor and Chair of Physiology and Biophysics; Director, Zilkha Neurogenetic Institute

centers had much earlier, by necessity, developed a culture of interdependence. As one professor who had previously worked at Stanford put it, "The ability to work across disciplines is real here—it's just lip service at other places."

When Scott Fraser, an eminent researcher in both biology and engineering at Caltech, announced in late 2012 that he would be moving to USC, it served particular notice that the university was now a destination for preeminent scholars who prized genuine interaction among disciplines.

In a major feature in *The Chronicle of Higher Education,* Fraser explained the process that led him to move from one of the world's most prestigious technical institutes to an up-and-coming university with more academic breadth. He had met with President Nikias and then-Provost Garrett.

"They asked me to dream big, and we talked about ways to get different disciplines to play nicely together. In those sorts of conversations, if they go

Peter Kuhn (left) and Raymond Stevens brought a 50-person team of researchers with them to USC from the Scripps Research Institute in late 2014 to focus on breakthroughs in convergent bioscience.

well, the candidate ends up recruiting himself." Fraser also said:

> USC is among only a handful of universities in the country that have the right range of departments and talents to do this. Caltech was an exceptional think tank and an institute where people could be fearless, but it's a small place, without a clinical presence. USC offers the possibility, on a single campus, of putting in place a program that could make it effortless for people to move from engineering to medicine or chemistry or whatever it takes to attack and solve a problem.

Fraser noted that he would be bringing a team of about two dozen with him from Caltech, and that he had already begun encouraging top researchers around the globe to join the converging scientific initiatives happening at USC.

The following spring, on a May morning in 2013, the academic and scientific worlds awoke to a seismic shift, when renowned scientists Arthur Toga and Paul Thompson announced that they would be relocating their famed Laboratory of Neuro Imaging to USC from crosstown rival UCLA. They brought with them a large team of world-class neuroscientists—about 110 faculty, researchers, and interdisciplinary staff.

Given the increasing importance of brain science, and the institute's potential to benefit a number of academic arenas, observers hailed the move as a coup for USC. As a front-page *Los Angeles Times* story observed:

> Scientists around the country said the move would further elevate USC, which recently has hired away professors and researchers from Caltech, Harvard, and other prestigious institutions.
>
> "It's a feather in USC's cap," said Dr. Bruce Rosen, director of a biomedical imaging center at Massachusetts General Hospital

> in Boston. He described the Toga-Thompson group as perhaps the world's premier lab when it comes to finding insights about the brain in massive amounts of data from scans and genetic tests.

In late 2014, USC recruited Raymond Stevens and Peter Kuhn, two leading scientists from the Scripps Research Institute, and with them, a 50-person team of researchers. Just as Fraser, Toga, and Thompson had seen an opportunity to take their research to a higher level by moving across town, Stevens and Kuhn saw greener academic fields farther up the 5 Freeway from Scripps's La Jolla setting.

In a *Chronicle of Higher Education* feature with the headline "Star by Star, Southern Cal Builds Strength in Bioscience," Stevens explained USC's appeal:

> Mr. Stevens says the lure for him, as for many other leading bioscientists, has been Southern California's emphasis on "convergent bioscience," a blend of biology, medicine, biotechnology, and engineering that corrects a trend that has persisted since Leonardo da Vinci drew his "Vitruvian Man" in about 1490: "Since that time, we've been dissecting science more and more and more," to now end up with 130 subdisciplines in medicine, 60 in biology, and 40 in chemistry, he says. "Now is the time to merge and bring all these things back together."

When neuroscience pioneers Arthur Toga (right) and Paul Thompson announced they would bring their Laboratory of Neuro Imaging and its world-class team of 110 researchers from UCLA to USC in 2013, it drew worldwide notice within the academic and scientific communities. The laboratory was later renamed the USC Mark and Mary Stevens Neuroimaging and Informatics Institute, thanks to a $50 million endowment gift from the university trustee and his wife.

Strength in Numbers

A number of key faculty recruitments involved large-scale hires of teams of scholars—senior and junior faculty, graduate students, and other researchers. The result was the instant establishment of academic strength in pioneering fields that combine aspects of biology, medicine, and engineering.

Andrew P. McMahon, Eli and Edythe Broad Center for Regenerative Medicine and Stem Cell Research: brought 12 researchers to USC

Raymond C. Stevens and Peter Kuhn, Biological Sciences: brought 50 researchers to USC

Paul M. Thompson and Arthur W. Toga, USC Mark and Mary Stevens Neuroimaging and Informatics Institute: brought 110 researchers to USC

Paul Aisen, USC Alzheimer's Therapeutic Research Institute: brought 30 researchers to USC

And Kuhn told the *Times of San Diego* that the university's skill in interdisciplinarity made the move a wise one, saying, "USC unites the best of the best, who align on the vision of improving human health."

The university celebrated another milestone in the summer of 2015, when Paul Aisen, a renowned researcher at UC San Diego, joined USC. He brought with him a team of 30 researchers and staff at the forefront of new approaches to Alzheimer's treatment. The university proudly announced the establishment of the USC Alzheimer's Therapeutic Research Institute in San Diego, with Aisen as its founding director and professor of neurology at the Keck School of Medicine.

Creative Sparks: New Hires in the Arts and Humanities

USC's lauded arts programs, housed mainly in six independent schools, have been key to infusing creative energy into its larger academic community. Accordingly, they were an important part of the university's recruiting effort.

Michael Tilson Thomas, a two-time graduate of USC's Thornton School of Music, returned in 2015 in the prestigious role of a Judge Widney Professor. A recipient of the National Medal of Arts, Tilson Thomas was the longtime music director of the San Francisco Symphony, as well as the principal guest conductor of the London Symphony Orchestra, and founder of the New World Symphony. At his alma mater, he would focus on teaching and mentoring students and helping them develop active professional careers.

The academic and art worlds both took note of two prominent

Glenn Dicterow, former concertmaster of the New York Philharmonic, and Karen Dreyfus, acclaimed violinist and faculty member at the Manhattan School of Music and the Juilliard School, joined the USC faculty in the fall of 2013.

USC hires in 2014—Glenn Dicterow, for many years the concertmaster of the New York Philharmonic, and his wife, Karen Dreyfus, a renowned musician who had taught at the Manhattan School of Music and the Juilliard School. Both brought with them not only enviable track records as professionals but reputations as skilled and inspiring instructors of young talent.

The university recruited the influential choreographer William Forsythe to be a part of the inaugural faculty for the USC Kaufman School of Dance, which welcomed its first class in the fall of 2015. The founder of the famed Forsythe Company dance troupe had deeply influenced ballet and contemporary dance throughout his long career. In his new role, Forsythe would

Transformative Faculty Recruitments: Arts and Humanities

Glenn Dicterow, Robert Mann Chair in Strings and Chamber Music; Professor of Violin
William Forsythe, Professor of Dance; Artistic Advisor, USC Choreographic Institute
Jodie Gates, Professor of Dance; Vice Dean and Director, USC Glorya Kaufman School of Dance
Frank Gehry, Judge Widney Professor of Architecture
Dana Gioia, Judge Widney Professor of Poetry and Public Culture
John Hawthorne, Professor of Philosophy
Sherman Jackson, King Faisal Chair in Islamic Thought and Culture; Professor of Religion and American Studies and Ethnicity
Amelia Jones, Robert A. Day Professor of Art and Design; Vice Dean of Critical Studies, USC Roski School of Art and Design
Claudia Rankine, Professor of English; Aerol Arnold Chair of English
Michael Tilson Thomas, Judge Widney Professor of Music
Gabriel Uzquiano Cruz, Professor of Philosophy
Ralph Wedgwood, Professor of Philosophy

USC: Nurturing of Academic Leaders 2010-2015

USC has been proud to nurture excellence in its academic leaders and executives, who are drawn from diverse scholarly disciplines. Many of these extraordinary individuals have gone on to leadership positions at the world's most preeminent universities and institutions.

TOP LEADERSHIP ROLES

Cornell University

Elizabeth Garrett, USC's provost and senior vice president for academic affairs from 2010–2015, became the first female president of Cornell in 2015.

UC Irvine

Howard Gillman, former USC vice provost and dean of USC Dornsife College, became the chancellor of UC Irvine in 2014.

Lewis & Clark College

Barry Glassner, former USC executive vice provost and professor of sociology, became the president of Lewis & Clark College in 2010.

Boston University

Jean Morrison, former USC vice provost for academic affairs, was named Boston University's provost and chief academic officer in 2011.

LEADERS IN ADVANCEMENT

American University: Courtney Surls, former USC vice president of development, was named vice president for development and alumni relations at American University in 2015.

Baylor University: David Rosselli, previously an executive director of development at USC, became vice president for university development at Baylor in 2015.

Carnegie Mellon University: Scott Mory, former director of USC's *Fas Regna Trojae* campaign, was appointed vice president for university advancement at CMU in 2015.

London School of Economics: Chris Yates, former USC advancement executive, became the director of LSE advancement in 2014.

MIT: Julie Lucas, former USC advancement executive, became vice president for resource development at MIT in 2014.

LEADERS IN ATHLETICS

Villanova University: Mark Jackson, formerly USC's senior associate director of athletics and chief innovation officer, was appointed director of athletics of Villanova in 2015.

Rutgers University: Paul Perrier, former USC associate vice president for athletic compliance, became senior associate athletic director/chief compliance officer at Rutgers in 2015.

University of Arizona: Kevin Sergent, formerly USC's director of athletic compliance, became UA's associate director of athletics for compliance in 2015.

teach undergraduates and also work with graduate students in the innovative International Artist Fellowship Program.

USC welcomed Christina Yu Yu, the former curator of Chinese and Korean art at the Los Angeles County Museum of Art (LACMA), to the director position at the USC Pacific Asia Museum in June of 2014. The *Los Angeles Times* published a major feature on Dr. Yu, noting the university's intentions to raise the museum to a higher level of influence and impact than before.

Within the humanities, USC's School of Philosophy showed explosive academic growth, thanks to several strategic "cluster" hires. It reached top-ten status in the view of many observers, with *Inside Higher Ed* reporting that on one well-respected ranking of graduate philosophy programs in 2013, the department had risen 35 places.

USC has recruited world-class faculty in recent years from virtually every field. Clockwise from top left: choreographer William Forsythe, one of the first professors at the USC Glorya Kaufman School of Dance; Dana Gioia, Widney Professor of Poetry and Public Culture; Dana Goldman, Leonard D. Schaeffer Chair and Director of the USC Schaeffer Center for Health Policy and Economics, with President Nikias; Jacob Soll, professor of history and accounting; and Paul Aisen, founding director of the USC Alzheimer's Therapeutic Research Institute.

Research of Consequence: New Hires in the Social Sciences and Professions

USC set out to be a template for high-impact, practical research in the social sciences and professions. Its leadership sought to bring a fresh approach to scholarship in these areas, to meaningfully inform policy makers, the media, and the general public as they work to find solutions to pressing challenges in the era of globalization. Accordingly, the university dramatically enhanced the influence and prominence of its social science and professional enterprises, including a number of key faculty additions.

Consistent with its overall strategy, USC made some of its high-level hires in this realm with an eye toward connecting the social sciences with the larger academic enterprise. Health economics was a significant example. Just as the university had announced its intention to increase its role in medicine and patient care, it was determined to play a larger role in the public-policy discussions that shape the development and delivery of health and medical services.

Toward that end, USC recruited the internationally acclaimed health economist Dana Goldman in 2009. Goldman previously worked at the RAND Corporation as the Distinguished Chair in Health Economics, directing its program in economics, finance, and organization while also serving on

Transformative Faculty Recruitments: Social Sciences and the Professions

Willow Bay, Professor of Professional Practice of Journalism; Director, USC School of Journalism

Dana Goldman, Leonard D. Schaeffer Director's Chair, USC Schaeffer Center for Health Policy and Economics; Professor of Public Policy, Pharmacy, and Economics

Andrew Guzman, Professor of Law; Carl Mason Franklin Dean's Chair in Law; Dean, USC Gould School of Law

James J. Heckman, Presidential Scholar-in-Residence, USC Schaeffer Center for Health Policy and Economics

Arie Kapteyn, Professor of Economics; Director, Center for Economic and Social Research

Daphna Oyserman, Dean's Professor of Psychology; Professor of Psychology, Education, and Communication

Norbert Schwarz, Provost Professor of Psychology and Marketing

Robert Shrum, Carmen H. and Louis Warschaw Chair in Practical Politics; Professor of the Practice of Political Science

Jacob Soll, Professor of History and Accounting

Arthur A. Stone, Professor of Psychology

the faculty of health services and radiology at UCLA. He now holds the titles of professor and the Leonard D. Schaeffer Director's Chair at USC. A team of other RAND scholars eventually joined Goldman at the USC Schaeffer Center in order to advance its mission to "measurably improve value in health through evidence based policy solutions, research excellence, transformative education, and private and public sector engagement."

Those key additions helped pave the way for future successes, such as the recruitment of the Nobel laureate economist Daniel McFadden from UC Berkeley in 2011. At USC, he was appointed to a Presidential Professorship of Health Economics, with joint positions at the USC Sol Price School of Public Policy and the department of economics within the Dornsife College.

President Nikias chats with Solomon Golomb, USC's acclaimed professor of engineering and mathematics. Golomb, who joined USC in 1963, is a University and Distinguished Professor, the Andrew and Erna Viterbi Chair in Communications, and a winner of the National Medal of Science.

McFadden and his colleague James Heckman had received the Nobel Prize in Economics in 2000 for their analysis of consumer behavior and its implications for public policy. Heckman was later named a Presidential Scholar-in-Residence at USC, in June 2015.

In another gain in the economics field, Jacob Soll joined the Trojans from Rutgers University in 2012. One of the world's most respected authorities on the emergence of the modern state and economic systems, he received joint appointments in the USC Leventhal School of Accounting and the Dornsife College history department. At Rutgers, Soll had been the winner of a $500,000 MacArthur Grant in 2011 for "opening up new fields of inquiry and elucidating how modern governments came into being." He has also been honored with a Guggenheim Fellowship, a Braudel Fellowship, a Jacques Barzun Prize in Cultural History, and a National Endowment for the Humanities Fellowship.

In 2014, USC recruited political luminary Robert Shrum as the inaugural Carmen H. and Louis Warschaw Chair in Practical Politics at the Dornsife College. The four-decade veteran of national politics came with a mission to engage students with opportunities to impact society—by working alongside public figures, elected officials, and campaigns spanning the ideological spectrum. "I think that we have one of the strongest political science departments in the country. But I also think our students need the tools to translate theory into action," Dean Steve A. Kay said of the appointment. "I believe Bob Shrum's experience and connections will serve to inspire students and to invigorate the department. I could not imagine anyone better to fill the Warschaw Chair and provide national recognition for our student programs in practical politics."

Raising the Profile: New Honors for Current Faculty

USC's shimmering constellations of new faculty superstars drew the eyes of the academic world. But strengthening its scholarly community required an

Increased Recognition for Top Faculty

In recent years, USC developed or expanded a number of designations recognizing special roles played by some of its most renowned and productive faculty—both current members and new recruits.

Provost Professors

A number of Provost Professorships were awarded by the provost to outstanding scholars who contribute to USC's culture of interdisciplinary research and education, and help attract high-level talent at the faculty and graduate student level.

New Appointments as of 2015:

Kate Flint, Provost Professor of English and Art History

Scott Fraser, Provost Professor of Biological Sciences and Biomedical Engineering

Henry Jenkins, Provost Professor of Communication, Journalism, and Cinematic Arts

Michael Kahn, Provost Professor of Medicine and Pharmacy

Pat Levitt, W. M. Keck Provost Professor of Neurogenetics, Neuroscience, Psychiatry, and Pharmacy

Andrew P. McMahon, W. M. Keck Provost Professor of Stem Cell Biology and Regenerative Medicine and Biological Sciences

Terence Sanger, Provost Associate Professor of Biomedical Engineering, Neurology, and Biokinesiology and Physical Therapy

Norbert Schwarz, Provost Professor of Psychology and Marketing

Raymond C. Stevens, Provost Professor of Biological Sciences and Chemistry

Arthur W. Toga, Provost Professor of Ophthalmology, Neurology, Psychiatry and the Behavioral Sciences, Radiology, and Biomedical Engineering

William Vega, Provost Professor of Social Work, Preventive Medicine, Psychiatry, Family Medicine, and Gerontology

Gary Watson, Provost Professor of Philosophy and Law

Wendy Wood, Provost Professor of Psychology and Business

Judge Widney Professors

Judge Widney Professorships are reserved for "eminent individuals from the arts, sciences, professions, business, and community and national leadership."

New Appointments as of 2015:

Frank Gehry, Judge Widney Professor of Architecture

Dana Gioia, Judge Widney Professor of Poetry and Public Culture

Daniel Hillis, Judge Widney Professor of Engineering and Medicine

Ray Irani, Judge Widney Professor of Chemical Engineering and Chemistry

General David Petraeus, Judge Widney Professor

Leonard Schaeffer, Judge Widney Professor and Chair

Ronald Sugar, Judge Widney Professor of Management and Technology

Michael Tilson Thomas, Judge Widney Professor of Music

Presidential Appointments

These special appointments were made by the university president to recognize figures of global stature who are now contributing to the USC academic community.

New Appointments as of 2015:

Murray Gell-Mann, Presidential Professor of Physics and Medicine

James Heckman, Presidential Scholar-in-Residence

Daniel McFadden, Presidential Professor of Health Economics

Gov. Arnold Schwarzenegger, Governor Downey Professor of State and Global Policy

equal commitment to supporting and promoting the work of the exceptional talents already on campus. To achieve these goals, the provost created a vice-provost position that would mentor scholars and lobby for external recognition and awards. In addition, USC's Office of Research Advancement, located just a few blocks from Capitol Hill in Washington, D.C., stepped up its efforts to aid the university's scholars fight for an increased share of the national research pie, helping to garner tens of millions of dollars in additional funding from federal agencies. Internally, millions of dollars in USC central administrative funding were directed to incentivize promising faculty work. Overall, the university was placing an increased priority on showcasing the work and legacies of its luminaries. The efforts very soon began to pay off, with accolades and press notices of USC faculty across all disciplines.

Honors in Science and Medicine

When Professor Arieh Warshel of the Dornsife College of Letters, Arts and Sciences won the 2013 Nobel Prize in Chemistry, it was a meaningful achievement for the university's academic community and larger Trojan Family. Warshel had spent decades at USC, and the prize validated the work that was performed daily on its campuses.

Just a few years earlier, there had been only one Nobel laureate on the USC faculty: George Olah, winner of the 1994 Nobel Prize in Chemistry. By 2015, there were five—an impressive increase by any measure.

Olah and his colleague G. K. Surya Prakash, both professors in the Dornsife College, were also honored in 2013, when they received the Eric and Sheila Samson Prime Minister's Prize for Innovation in Alternative Fuels for Transportation from the State of Israel. The $1 million prize recognized their pioneering research in advancing methanol markets and their work in developing viable emerging energy sources.

In the same year, University Professor and Distinguished Professor Solomon Golomb, a faculty member in the USC Viterbi School's Ming Hsieh Department of Electrical Engineering, was presented with the nation's highest honor for scientific innovation, the National Medal of Science, at the White House. And the academic community celebrated the election of 15 USC faculty to the American Association for the Advancement of Science. These members came from both of the university's major campuses, representing the Dornsife College, the Viterbi School of Engineering, the Keck School of Medicine, and the Davis School of Gerontology.

Arieh Warshel receives the 2013 Nobel Prize in Chemistry from King Carl XVI Gustaf of Sweden in Stockholm. A member of USC's faculty for four decades, Warshel developed computational models to simulate and explore a vast range of complex chemical and biological interactions.

Professor Jae U. Jung, chair of the department of molecular microbiology and immunology, received South Korea's 2012 Ho-Am Prize in Medicine, one of that nation's highest honors. Jung, who came to USC in 2007 from Harvard Medical School, has become a preeminent expert in the molecular biology of gamma-herpes viruses and their gene products as they relate to biochemistry, cell biology, and immunology.

News outlets around the world in 2013 and 2014 featured Professor Mark Humayun's breakthrough research that was paving the way to partially restore sight to the blind in some circumstances. The work of Humayun's team was a collaboration between engineering, biology, and medicine—a tangible

sign of the miracles within reach of USC's academic community.

Continuing throughout 2014, honors and recognition for USC faculty were in no small supply. *Los Angeles Magazine* hailed Professor Roberta Diaz Brinton—the R. Pete Vanderveen Chair in Therapeutic Discovery and Development at the USC School of Pharmacy—as its "Woman of the Year," in honor of her groundbreaking research into Alzheimer's disease. Brinton developed two compounds, currently in clinical trials, that have extraordinary potential to address this progressive condition, which currently afflicts more than 5 million people in the United States alone.

That year three USC Viterbi faculty were included on the prestigious *MIT Technology Review*'s list of "Innovators Under 35": Professor George Ban-Weiss, as a humanitarian who has contributed to climate research; Professor Megan McCain, as an innovator who advances personalized cardiac

medicines; and Professor Maryam Shanechi, as a pioneer who uses control theory to understand the brain.

That same year, *Fortune* magazine included Professor Tracy Fullerton on its list of "Ten Powerful Women in Video Games." Professor Vaughn Starnes made *The Hollywood Reporter*'s list of "Hollywood's Top Doctors" in the area of thoracic and cardiovascular surgery. And *Popular Science* included Professor Andrea Armani among the year's "Brilliant Ten," recognizing her passionate pursuit of innovation and her contributions to scientific discovery, notably through sensors she developed that function like an optical tuning fork and may help detect extremely elusive traces of disease.

Honors in the Arts and Humanities

Acclaimed historian Kevin Starr of the Dornsife College of Letters, Arts and Sciences received the Robert Kirsch Award for Lifetime Achievement at the 2013 *Los Angeles Times* Book Prizes. Starr had previously received numerous

Tracy Fullerton, professor of cinematic arts and director of the USC Game Innovation Lab, gained international acclaim for her work as a game designer, entrepreneur, and the author of *Game Design Workshop*, a text on game design used around the world.

Broadcast journalist and new-media innovator Willow Bay stands before the state-of-the-art Jacki and Gilbert Cisneros Assignment Desk in the Julie Chen/Leslie Moonves and CBS Media Center. Bay arrived in 2014 to serve as director of the USC School of Journalism within the USC Annenberg School for Communication and Journalism.

honors, including the National Humanities Medal in a ceremony at the White House. In 2015, the Robert Kirsch Award went to renowned novelist T. C. Boyle, a writer in residence and Distinguished Professor Emeritus of English at USC.

In 2012, highly prestigious Guggenheim Fellowships were awarded to Stanya Kahn, adjunct faculty at the Roski School of Art and Design, and Brighde Mullins, director of the Master of Professional Writing program at the Dornsife College. Violinist Midori Goto of the Thornton School of Music, already one of the jewels in USC's arts crown, was elected to the American Academy of Arts and Sciences in 2013. The following year, the Los Angeles Master Chorale offered a major performance tribute to USC Distinguished Professor Morten Lauridsen, a 2007 National Medal of Arts winner whose seminal works include "O Magnum Mysterium."

The *Los Angeles Times* spotlighted many other USC faculty in the arts, including a profile on theater legend Gordon Davidson (the founder of the Mark Taper Forum and former artistic director of Center Theatre Group) and actor and writer Eric Trules. Together they taught a semester-long seminar at the USC School of Dramatic Arts.

Academy Award-winning cinematic arts professor Paul Debevec, who

helped create a new visual language in the movie *Avatar*, continued to gain acclaim. A notable example was an in-depth 2014 piece in *The New Yorker* on his work at the USC Institute for Creative Technologies, examining the pioneering use of animation techniques and the creation of lifelike digital models.

And legendary School of Cinematic Arts alumnus and benefactor George Lucas, who now holds a presidential appointment on the USC faculty, received the National Medal of Arts in a White House ceremony in 2013.

Honors in Social Sciences and Professions

University Professor Manuel Castells received Norway's 2012 Holberg International Memorial Prize, a $775,000 award that recognizes outstanding

At the 2014 USC-Stanford football game, the university honored members of its academic community who have won National Medals of Distinction, which are awarded at the White House. From left: then-Provost Elizabeth Garrett, University Professor Kevin Starr, alumnus and Trustee Andrew Viterbi, Distinguished Professor Morten Lauridsen, University and Distinguished Professor Solomon Golomb, and President Nikias.

University Professor Manuel Castells, here with President Nikias, is the world's most cited scholar in the field of communications. In 2012, he received Norway's Holberg International Memorial Prize, one of academia's most prestigious awards.

scholarly work in the arts and humanities, social sciences, law, and theology. Castells is the most cited communication scholar in the world, and holds the Wallis Annenberg Chair of Communication Technology and Society at USC. The award committee, calling him the "leading sociologist of the city and new information and media technologies," recognized him for work completed entirely during his tenure at USC, which began in 2003.

Ernest J. Wilson III, dean of the Annenberg School for Communication and Journalism, has been active in guiding diplomacy and policy development at the national and international levels. In 2012, he was elected a member of the American Academy of Arts and Sciences, bringing the number of living AAAS Fellows among the USC faculty to 27, in addition to five members on the university's Board of Trustees.

Fittingly, an array of media outlets reported on the 2014 appointment of the new director of the Annenberg School of Journalism: Willow Bay, a veteran television news anchor and *Huffington Post* executive. Coverage noted that she came to the school just as it was opening Wallis Annenberg Hall, an 88,000-square-foot facility designed to reinvent journalism for the next era.

Also in that year, then-Provost Elizabeth Garrett was elected to the governing body of the American Law Institute, a prominent organization that promotes legal reform and advocates for improvements in the law. An elected

In 2014, Ginger Clark, associate professor of clinical education in the Rossier School of Education, became the first faculty member outside the traditional tenure track to preside over the USC Academic Senate. Her election reflected the expanding role of these scholars in the life and governance of the larger academic community.

member of the ALI since 2008, she became the only university provost on the council at the time. Not long afterward, Garrett was named president-elect of Cornell University.

Encouraging Excellence in Junior Faculty

At the same time USC's leadership was seeking to support and boost the work of its senior faculty, the Office of the Provost expanded campus-wide efforts to nurture scholarship and research by junior and underrepresented faculty members.

Among such initiatives, the Provost's Assistant Professor Fellowship provides crucial one-year funds to support junior faculty members' work ahead of their tenure review, also with an eye on assisting candidates from underrepresented backgrounds. And the Center for Excellence in Teaching offers both junior and senior faculty in every discipline resources to improve methods for teaching in a learner-centered environment.

Many USC faculty members in the early stages of their careers have received recent accolades:

- Gian-Maria Annovi, assistant professor of French and Italian and gender studies, received a grant in 2015 from the Creative Capital/Andy Warhol Foundation Arts Writers Grant Program.
- Sabela Grimes, assistant professor of practice in dance, was named a 2014 United States Artists Rockefeller Fellow.
- Sarah Gualtieri, associate professor of American studies and ethnicity, history, and Middle East studies, was named a National Endowment for the Humanities Fellow in 2015.
- Hao Li, assistant professor of computer science, was named to *MIT Technology Review*'s "35 Innovators Under 35" list in 2013.
- Megan Luke, assistant professor of art history, received the 2015 Robert Motherwell Book Award.
- Ellis Meng, professor and chair of biomedical engineering, was recognized in 2009 as one of *MIT Technology Review*'s "35 Innovators Under 35." She also was a recipient of the National Science Foundation CAREER and Wallace H. Coulter Foundation Early Career awards.

- Viet Thanh Nguyen, associate professor of English, American studies, and ethnicity, received the 2015 Center for Fiction First Novel Prize.
- Olu Orange, adjunct assistant professor of political science, received a 2015 *California Lawyer* Attorney of the Year (CLAY) Award.
- Jennifer Swift, associate professor of spatial sciences, was a 2015–2016 inductee into the VIP Woman of the Year Circle of the National Association of Professional Women.

Approaching Critical Mass

Since 2010, Nikias had spoken of strengthening USC's academic enterprise in a variety of metaphors—for instance, completing a metamorphosis, achieving critical mass, increasing the university's gravitas, and bringing new opportunities into its orbit. The common theme involved the notion that a bold, urgent yet strategic approach could change the game rapidly. It would allow for dramatic academic progress, in which the whole would exceed the constituent pieces in scope, scale, and impact. Within a few short years, the evolving profile of the faculty hinted that massive transformation—and that elusive critical mass—was within reach.

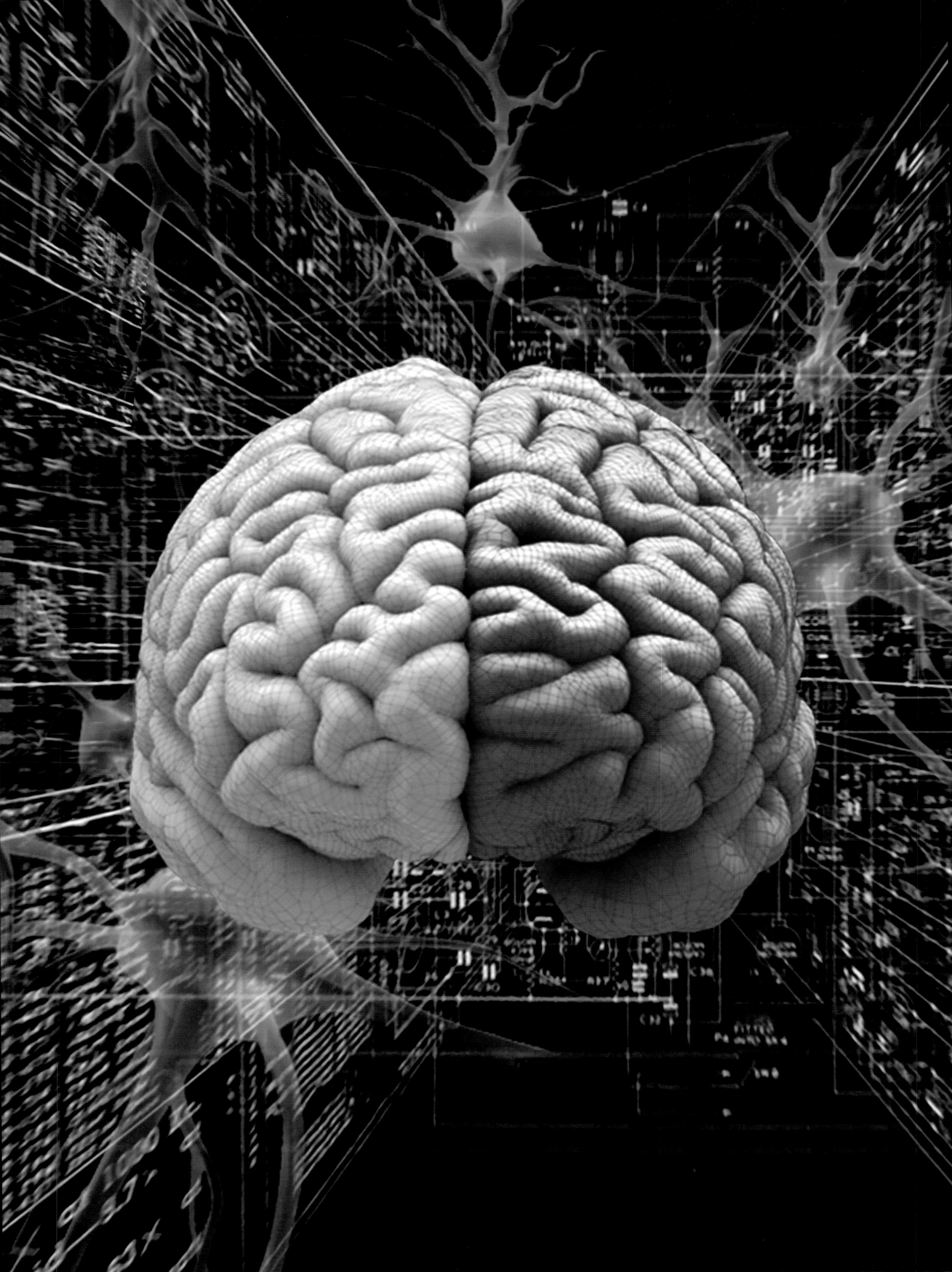

Chapter 5

The Adventure of Discovery

USC Advances on New Frontiers

Since President Norman H. Topping placed USC on a path as a research university in the 1960s, it has taken this role seriously and with pride. While traditional colleges see their role as transmitting existing knowledge, leading research universities make it their goal to test that accumulated learning, and to create knowledge along the way. The result is that the entire campus community—from freshmen to senior faculty—is immersed in an environment of discovery, and the larger society benefits from the subsequent innovation.

By 1969, USC had been elected to the Association of American Universities, the consortium of leading North American research institutions. This milestone has helped USC's faculty drive revolutions in cinematic arts, aerospace, personal computing, the Internet, and other key emerging areas.

Zohrab Kaprielian, who joined USC as an engineering faculty member in 1958, deserves considerable credit for the university's stunning progress in its early years as a bona fide research institution. As an administrator and dean at the USC Viterbi School, and later as the university's executive vice president, he recruited rising young faculty stars, including George Olah (who would become USC's first Nobel laureate decades later), Solomon Golomb, and Irving Reed—all of whom would go on to earn international distinction as pioneers in emerging fields. Kaprielian established key alliances with government and industry and, in 1972, brought to USC the famed Information Sciences Institute, which helped give shape to the Internet and the entire digital age.

Building academic strengths where competing institutions were weak, and utilizing USC's unique assets to shrewdly make the most of its advantages, Kaprielian perhaps created the template that future administrations would follow to great effect.

Like Kaprielian, C. L. Max Nikias arrived at USC as a faculty member in electrical engineering—and as an avid champion of the power of university

USC faculty, with a fresh infusion of some of the world's best scholarly talent, moved into leadership positions on some of the most important intellectual frontiers of this century, including neuroscience and the interdisciplinary study of the brain.

research to drive societies and economies forward. To boost its research capacity and national standing, USC's leaders tapped Nikias early on to lead an ambitious effort to win an Engineering Research Center (or "Center of Excellence") that would be funded by the National Science Foundation. After several years of patient alliance building and planning, overcoming obstacles along the way, Nikias and his colleagues succeeded with a proposal to the NSF that beat out those from research giants like UC Berkeley, Michigan, and 115 other institutions. USC's Integrated Multimedia Systems Center (IMSC), established in 1996, would be home to the country's first national multimedia research center.

The Collaborative High Altitude Flow Facility (CHAFF) chamber, part of the USC Viterbi School of Engineering, can be cryogenically cooled to below -300 degrees Fahrenheit. The cold walls of the chamber maintain a simulated space environment by condensing and trapping thruster exhaust gases.

Annette Kim (second from left) was recruited from MIT to head USC's Spatial Analysis Teaching Laboratory (SATLAB) and Spatial Analysis Lab (SLAB). In the spring of 2015, she taught the first class in the SATLAB, titled "Urban Spatial Ethnography and Critical Cartography."

That achievement set the stage for the university to punch above its weight, in research terms, on multiple occasions in the following years. Nikias went on to serve as associate dean of the USC Viterbi School and became dean in 2001. He worked alongside Professor Mark Humayun to establish still another NSF-funded Center of Excellence, the Engineering Research Center for Biomimetic MicroElectronic Systems (known as BMES), which allowed USC to leap forward in the crucial, nascent field of biotechnology. And working with Viterbi professor Randolph Hall (who would eventually become USC's vice president of research), Nikias established the National Center for Risk and Economic Analysis of Terrorism Events (CREATE), the first Center of Excellence to be funded by the Department of Homeland Security.

By the time Nikias was elevated to provost in 2005—having mentored Humayun, Hall, and others successfully in their efforts to build top research programs—he was determined to broaden and expand the ways in which USC faculty in every field could create innovative cross-disciplinary research alliances.

American research universities had drawn criticism in the prior years, especially due to the high costs of building and maintaining state-of-the-art laboratories and the devotion of many senior faculty to research and discovery

rather than to classroom teaching. While acknowledging that research universities needed to make changes, Nikias, as USC's provost, offered a spirited defense of the institutions and their work, arguing that they were the key reason that the world's best minds moved to the United States and thereby benefited the national economy and society.

In his 2009 Pullias Lecture at the USC Rossier School of Education, he argued that the academic community at a great American research university was uniquely gifted to bring new light to society—in much the same way that the legendary titan Prometheus stole fire from the gods and delivered it to a humanity lurking in darkness:

> These are the modern Prometheans, storming Mount Olympus in order to encounter Athena and the wisdom she offers, in order to find fire, and in order to bring those blessings back to humanity.
>
> And these persons cannot be headquartered anywhere. They are at home only in an environment that encourages collaboration across disciplines, that encourages experimentation, that allows them to make mistakes over and over, and then to start fresh the next morning. Can the modern corporation allow such an environment? Can a government laboratory? Of course not—only the American research university can.

Clockwise from top left: Alexander McDowell of the USC School of Cinematic Arts has been one of the most influential scholars in the area of narrative media; Laurie Eisenberg of the Keck School of Medicine of USC has advanced research in auditory perception, pediatric hearing loss, and the development of sensory devices; Leslie A. Saxon, also of the Keck School of Medicine, has guided progress in cardiology and the development of cardiac devices and wireless health systems; and Daphna Oyserman of USC Dornsife has detailed how small factors create significant differences in educational and healthcare outcomes.

> Our American research universities indeed have fire to capture, and to carry forward to humanity, to warm it and to enlighten it and to enliven it.

In a presidential address to the faculty a few years later, Nikias would again visit the theme of finding new intellectual light—and how USC was poised to play a special role in a thrilling next age of enlightenment:

> For the faculty of USC, this continues to be our moment. It is in times such as these—moments of disruption—in which we see the most promising developments. These are moments of new light, a re-illumination of the human mind and spirit.
>
> In the Late Middle Ages, Petrarch ignited one moment of re-illumination, when the first wave of humanists took accumulated wisdom and the classics, and used them to spark a new intellectual encounter, and to brighten our understanding of humanity's place in the cosmos. Francis Bacon would later fashion modern notions of rigorous, empirical inquiry. In his monumental book the *Novum Organum,* human inquiry smashed through ancient barriers, opening vast new worlds for exploration.
>
> Our own world is opening up, in the 21st century, in no less dramatic ways.... This is the Age of the Pacific—and yes, this is the century of biology and medicine. In this era, human inquiry is being informed by the extraordinary convergence of Pacific Rim cultures, by the rich blending of a new world into the existing one.
>
> This is an era in which the crucial issues of how we live, and how well we live, and how long we live will be illuminated by creative and collaborative adventurers across the sciences and engineering, the humanities, the arts and social sciences, and the professions. As a private, comprehensive research powerhouse, here at the greatest cultural and commercial crossroads of the Pacific Rim, USC finds circumstances working in its favor. Located in this place, at this time, with our unique assets, we find that destiny has dealt us a favorable hand. Let us play this out wisely.

The Interdisciplinary Advantage

In recent years, information technology and immersive, digital media have begun to reshape the landscape in education and every realm that involves human communication. The university's faculty was again determined to play a significant role.

Interdisciplinarity was by now the watchword within American higher education. It was recognized almost universally that the greatest intellectual breakthroughs would happen at the borders and bridges of different academic disciplines—in contrast to the manner of narrow hyper-specialization that had characterized the last century of scholarly inquiry. Here, USC's many

President Barack Obama poses in front of a light stage in 2014 so that USC's Institute for Creative Technologies researchers can create 3-D portraits of him for the Smithsonian Institution. The project is overseen by Paul Debevec, ICT's chief visual officer and a research professor in the USC Viterbi computer science department.

This two-dimensional photo is one of a multitude of images that ICT combined to create its full, 3-D image of President Obama.

independent but interdependent schools represented an invaluable mix of breadth and depth. With humanities, sciences, arts, social sciences, and professions frequently working together, the university's faculty moved swiftly into uncharted academic territories.

"I'm proud of the fact that USC has not been copying anyone else or chasing anyone else in this area," Nikias told the faculty in his annual State of the University address in early 2014. "USC has been experimenting and exploring, and has been leading the way for others."

A capacity for interdisciplinary approaches would prove especially useful in pushing forward new frontiers, particularly those that involved both technological and human aspects. "Big data" was one such example.

By 2010, big data had emerged in the public consciousness as a formidable concept. This growing field will allow information to assume an even more imposing and hopefully constructive presence in the world, allowing societies to make intelligent decisions based on solid data, rather than on hunches, biases, ideologies, or wishful thinking.

"Given the role that our faculty and students have played in the information revolution so far, USC is poised to lead the 'big data' era," said Provost Michael Quick, in the spring of 2015. "Big data has implications

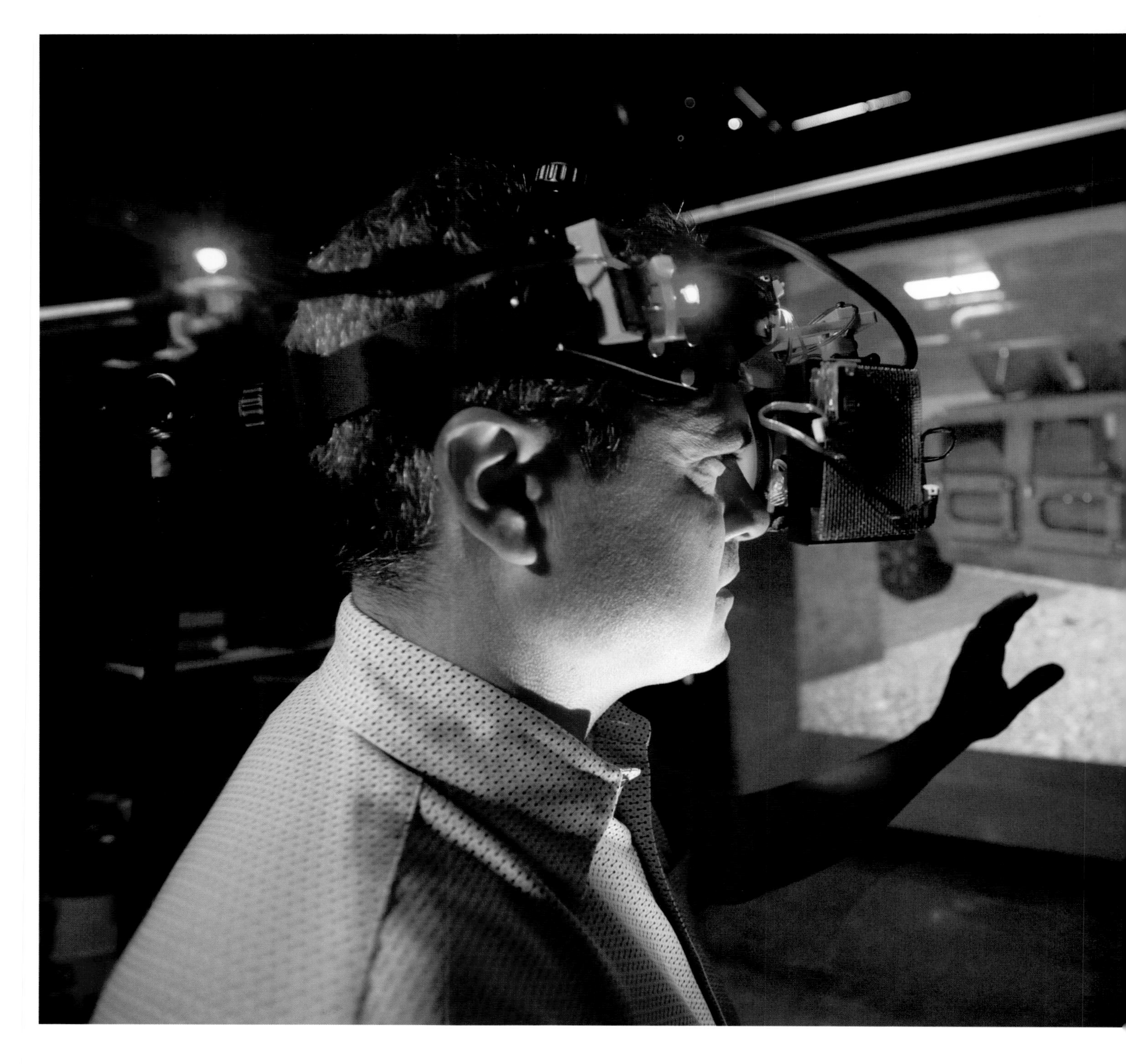

for communications, health and medicine, the arts and humanities, and seemingly every aspect of human life. So it's one of those areas where our faculty can truly play a shaping role."

The Viterbi School of Engineering, the Dornsife College, the School of Cinematic Arts, the Annenberg School for Communication and Journalism, and the Keck School of Medicine all represented strong assets in USC's effort to shape the development of big data. In 2014, the university received a landmark National Institutes of Health Big Data to Knowledge Grant—about $23 million for two new Centers of Excellence. That constituted 20 percent of the entire nation's investment in big data. It came on the heels of a $16 million National Institute of Mental Health grant a month earlier; together, the

USC researchers from numerous disciplines have worked through ICT to develop virtual-reality and virtual-human technologies that help train U.S. military personnel for more effective service.

awards served as proof that USC's faculty could both compete and win in an increasingly uncertain federal funding environment.

Scholarship of Consequence

Elizabeth Garrett, USC's provost from 2010 to 2015, encouraged the faculty to focus on "scholarship of consequence," which can meaningfully shape and improve the workings of society. This principle guided the development of Dr. Verna and Peter Dauterive Hall, which opened in 2014 to serve as an intellectual crossroads that would stimulate social science scholarship and meaningfully inform public policy discussions. Dauterive Hall became host to four centers with precisely that objective:

- The Center for Economic and Social Research, which focuses on the behavioral sciences and related areas;
- The USC Schwarzenegger Institute for State and Global Policy, which explores post-partisan policy approaches;
- The USC Dornsife Mind and Society Center, which takes a scholarly and empirical approach to examining the manner in which human minds and society shape one another; and
- The Leonard D. Schaeffer Center for Health Policy and Economics, which explores the economic and human dimensions of healthcare delivery.

The Schaeffer Center was created in 2009 through a major gift from Leonard and Pamela Schaeffer. Its mission is, by utilizing an unusual breadth and depth of expertise, to improve healthcare through evidence-based policy solutions that could transcend conventional partisan bickering. The university recruited the eminent health economist Dana Goldman to lead the center, which would combine insights from faculty within USC's Price School of Public Policy, School of Pharmacy, and other units.

Technology for a Human Purpose

As with so many other aspects of USC's academic rise, the rapid growth of its research enterprise was enabled by collaboration within widely disparate fields. This involved scholarly partnerships among the sciences, social sciences, arts, humanities, and professions.

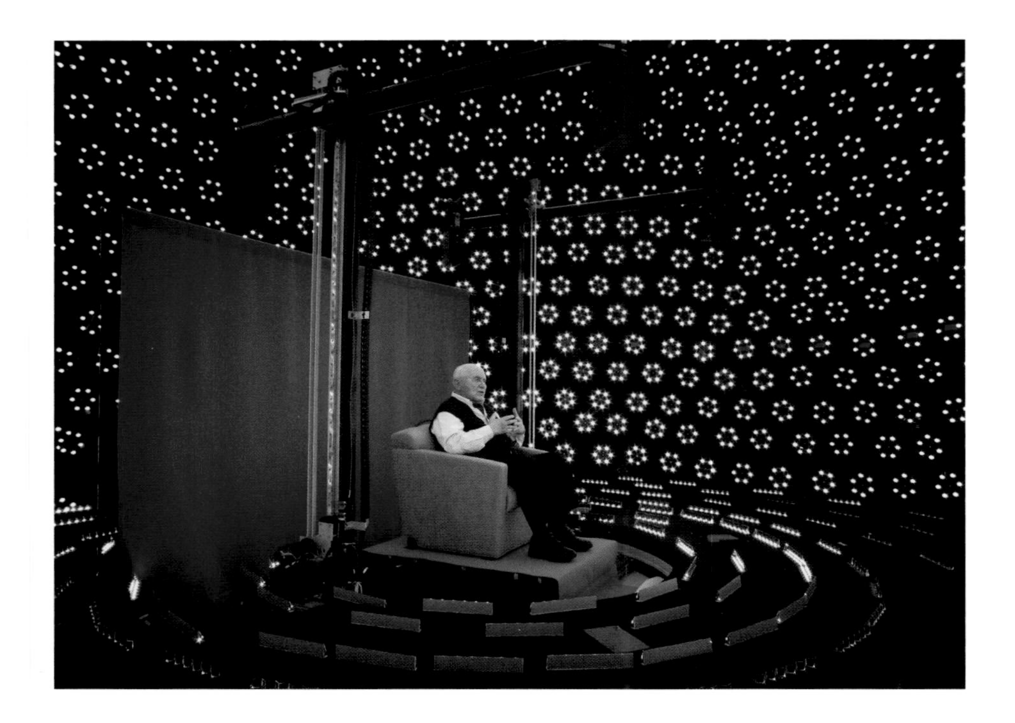

Through the aid of innovative cinematic technologies, the USC Shoah Foundation has been able to create enduring encounters with survivors of the Holocaust.

Audience members at the Shoah Foundation interact with a 3-D holographic rendering of an individual survivor. After hearing his story, they can ask specific questions about his experiences, to which the holographic subject retrieves and articulates pre-recorded answers in real time.

Observers have noted the gradual marginalization of the humanities at many American research universities in recent decades, but the USC faculty has moved to revitalize scholarship in this area, launching a public humanities initiative in order to connect the work of numerous scholars to pressing issues of the day. Alice Villaseñor, an expert on 19th-century British literature and women writers, took on the role of director of the initiative.

In 2014, the Andrew W. Mellon Foundation awarded the university a $1.9 million grant for the USC Digital Humanities Program, which will train graduate and postdoctoral students in key academic areas at the intersection of the humanities, technology, and the social sciences.

"We're at a really early phase," said Peter Mancall, vice dean for the humanities at the USC Dornsife College and principal investigator for the grant. "The digital humanities can embrace new ways of doing research. Part of doing this project will be to figure out what those ways actually are." Other faculty leaders for the program include Philip Ethington, professor of history, political science, and spatial sciences within USC Dornsife, and Tara McPherson, associate professor of critical studies at the School of Cinematic Arts.

Additional innovations in humanities scholarship involved the development of disciplines such as sound studies, an interdisciplinary field that

examines the sonic elements of history and culture. Joshua Kun, a professor in the USC Annenberg School for Communication and Journalism, became active within both sound studies—especially the study of popular music—and the university's public humanities initiative, curating exhibits and editing non-academic books, among other projects.

The Convergence of Technology, Entertainment, and Education

USC's Institute for Creative Technologies has been at the forefront of the development of "virtual humans" and "virtual environments" for educational purposes. ICT was created in 1999 with funding from the United States Army. In 2011, the Army extended its partnership with ICT, through $135 million in funding over the next three years.

At USC's 2014 Global Conversation in New York, Provost Professor Scott Fraser discusses interdisciplinary work that can prevent blindness in many patients.

As in so many cases involving university-government partnerships, the work began with a national security dimension, then branched out into all realms of society. ICT enabled trainers to use virtual-human technologies to equip more than 75,000 soldiers for combat, negotiation, and diplomacy, as well as recovery from post-traumatic stress and brain injuries.

At the same time, Paul Debevec, ICT's chief visual officer and a Viterbi professor, was working with his colleagues at ICT to create virtual worlds and new 3-D images for Hollywood, notably in the landmark film *Avatar*. And as video gaming promised to become far bigger and widespread than cinematic entertainment had ever been, ICT researchers took state-of-the-art gaming concepts to a higher level, for the purposes of both education and entertainment.

One of the more poignant marriages of technology and the humanities is demonstrated in the work of the USC Shoah Foundation—The Institute for Visual History and Education. The foundation has archived and organized 53,000 testimonies from Holocaust survivors in order to teach and connect with a broad audience of people in the coming generations. Working with partners at ICT, and the concept developer Conscience Display, Shoah has invented unique ways to bring the Visual History Archive to life.

The team began by capturing detailed, extended interviews with

Holocaust survivors using special technologies that present each subject in 3-D holographic form. These interviews were then combined with an interactive component that can hear a question from a member of the audience and—in real time—provide an appropriate sound bite from the interviewee. For instance, a schoolchild might ask, "Did you ever see your family again?" and the holographic image would, in an instant, move to that part of his or her story.

Stephen D. Smith, the executive director of the USC Shoah Foundation, explained their goal: that the content "must be natural language video conversations rendered in true holographic display, without 3-D glasses."

Reflecting on these emerging technologies, Nikias commented, "All this just hints at the incredible future of storytelling and the future of teaching and learning. And these virtual experiences are increasingly available by mobile devices, anywhere, anytime. The only limit to all these possibilities is our own imagination."

To CREATE a More Secure World

The United States Department of Homeland Security established the National Center for Risk and Economic Analysis of Terrorism Events (CREATE) at USC in 2004, to allow a coalition of universities and research institutions to assess and address security threats to the nation. In the fall of 2010, DHS renewed its relationship with CREATE with a $15.3 million grant.

CREATE teams have developed strategies for making security checkpoints and patrols more effective; improved security processes for the Los Angeles and Long Beach ports (the busiest in the nation); modeled economic resilience following a catastrophic regional event; and explored the links between threats, disasters, and human behavioral responses. Along the way they have also produced hundreds of articles, book chapters, reports, and other publications advancing scholarship in this field.

Powering the Health Revolution

USC entered the second decade of this century determined to be a leader in the burgeoning revolution in healthcare and the biological sciences. In order to do so, it needed to connect its strong programs in engineering, medicine, health, and other areas and leverage them more fully. This led to several academic success stories in short order.

The Engineering Research Center for Biomimetic MicroElectronic Systems (BMES) was established in 2003 with $17 million in funding from the National Science Foundation. Based at USC, it represented the alliance of a number of important business and academic institutions, including Caltech and UC Santa Cruz. Both USC officials and local civic leaders believed the center had significant potential to move Southern California to the vanguard of the rising biotech industry.

BMES is led by biomedical engineer and ophthalmologist Mark Humayun, who worked with Nikias during the latter's time as engineering dean to establish the center. It aimed for unprecedented breakthroughs in the treatment of blindness, cognitive decline, paralysis, and loss of neuromuscular control. When Professor Humayun and his colleagues announced in 2013 the development of an artificial retina that restored partial sight in some blind patients, the news quickly traveled around the world.

The BMES center is just one key component of a major USC effort to drive research breakthroughs in health and medicine. Broadly strengthening the faculty has been an even more urgent priority. University officials, led by President Nikias, former Provost Garrett, and, now, Provost Michael Quick, wooed some of the world's best talent to build preeminent centers in major fields.

Andrew McMahon came from Harvard in 2012 to serve as the chair of the newly created department of stem cell biology and regenerative medicine at the Keck School, and director of the Eli and Edythe Broad Center for Regenerative Medicine and Stem Cell Research at USC. He also received an appointment in the department of biological sciences in USC Dornsife, symbolizing the university's attention to cross-disciplinary approaches that integrate both of its major campuses.

Scott Fraser, a pacesetter in both biology and engineering research at Caltech, came to USC in 2012 as Provost Professor of Biological Sciences, Biomedical Engineering, Physiology and Biophysics, Stem Cell Biology and Regenerative Medicine, Pediatrics, Radiology and Ophthalmology. As the many areas of specialty in his title indicate, his mission was to put the assets

Clockwise from top left: Andrea Armani of the USC Viterbi School of Engineering explores the interaction of light and biology, with implications for biomedical devices; Kevin Knight of USC's Information Sciences Institute has developed new approaches to cryptography, code breaking, and artificial intelligence; and Ellis Meng, also of USC Viterbi, was named to *MIT Technology Review*'s list of top innovators for breakthroughs in next-generation drug-delivery pumps.

of a broad, interdisciplinary research institution to work in what he called an "exciting effort to build a new convergence of fields."

Arthur Toga and Paul Thompson brought their elite Laboratory of Neuro Imaging (LONI) to the university from UCLA in 2013, and along with it a team of 110 top-flight researchers and staff. The following year, Raymond Stevens and Peter Kuhn joined USC, along with their 50-member team from Scripps Research Institute, to make faster progress in molecular biology.

Translating Ideas into Innovation

Too often, no tangible societal benefit comes from brilliant ideas that arise within an academic community. USC, entrepreneurial in nature since its earliest days, made a determined effort to make sure that ideas could be translated into beneficial innovation. The USC Stevens Center for Innovation, established in 2004 by a $22 million gift from Trustee Mark Stevens and his wife, Mary, catalyzed the process of spurring innovation across both university campuses. USC Stevens gave faculty a well-staffed, well-equipped ally that could protect their intellectual property; allow them to benefit from it; and help them develop it into promising products and services that could make a real difference in the world.

By 2015, some 70 companies had been founded using the USC Stevens Center for Innovation, which attracted more than $355 million in venture capital funding. Licensing revenue increased from $3.2 million in 2007 to $6.5 million by 2015.

Promoting Diversity in Science and Engineering

The university has made a concerted effort to support women and underrepresented minorities in its research departments. The USC Women in Science & Engineering (WiSE) program, leveraging a $20 million endowment and founded by former vice provost Jean Morrison, develops greater diversity among faculty and students within these fields. Viterbi School of Engineering professor Maja Matarić, who has been named one of the 25 most powerful women in technology by *Business Insider*, has played a prominent leadership and mentoring role within WiSE.

Among several indications of the program's success: Women now comprise roughly 38 percent of the freshmen class at USC Viterbi—about double the national average. And six women on the engineering school's faculty have been named to *MIT Technology Review*'s annual lists of "Top 35 Global Innovators Under 35" since 2009.

Included in these honorees were professors Maryam Shanechi and

Clockwise from top left: Michael Habib of the Keck School of Medicine has detailed the development of large feathered dinosaurs, pterosaurs, and the origin of flight in birds; Julie M. Zissimopoulos of the USC Price School has earned acclaim for her research into the economics of aging and new approaches to healthcare policy; Theodore Berger of the USC Viterbi School has drawn notice for his work in the neurophysiology of memory and learning; and Maryam Shanechi and Bhaskar Krishnamachari, also of USC Viterbi, were named to *Popular Science*'s 2015 "Brilliant 10" list for their work on neurological interfaces and wireless networks, respectively.

Clockwise from top left: Maja Matarić has developed advanced robotic devices while also nurturing academic diversity and mentoring junior faculty members; Roberta Diaz Brinton has gained national attention for her studies of Alzheimer's disease and the effects of drugs on the human brain, and for developing treatments to prevent and remedy memory disorders; Hao Li gained renown as an expert in CGI, 3-D digitization, animation, and motion-picture technology; and Elizabeth Currid-Halkett of the Price School has driven progress in scholarship involving urban planning and social networks, while also exploring the economic impact of art and culture.

Bhaskar Krishnamachari of the Viterbi School's Ming Hsieh Department of Electrical Engineering. In the fall of 2015, both were also named to *Popular Science*'s annual "Brilliant 10" list. In 2013, Andrea Armani, the Fluor Early Career Chair in Engineering, was also recognized in that ranking.

The university makes a point of recruiting exceptional early-career faculty members from other institutions. Daphna Oyserman, who received a W. T. Grant Faculty Scholar Award and a Humboldt Scientific Contribution Prize from the German Alexander von Humboldt Foundation, came to USC from the University of Michigan in 2013 as a Dean's Professor of Psychology, and professor of psychology, education, and communication.

Julie Zissimopoulos, formerly a senior economist at the RAND Corporation, now serves as associate director of USC's Leonard D. Schaeffer Center for Health Policy and Economics. She is also a network associate of the MacArthur Foundation's Research Network on an Aging Society, and co-directs the Resource Center for Minority Aging Research (funded by the National Institute on Aging).

Student Research Opportunities

In recent years, higher education experts have seen America's universities as overly focused on research at the expense of undergraduate teaching. USC,

Billed as the world's leading undergraduate rocket research group, USC's Rocket Propulsion Laboratory has steadily progressed toward its goal of sending the first rocket designed and built by students to the boundary of space.

by contrast, has moved to underscore how student-faculty collaborations can offer unique educational opportunities to create knowledge.

During Nikias's tenure as provost, the university introduced the Discovery Scholars program to incentivize students across every discipline to participate actively with faculty in creating original academic and artistic works. The Discovery Scholar designation, granted annually at commencement, was bestowed upon 70 graduating seniors in the spring of 2015. Ten of those students received $10,000 awards for the most exceptional work.

As dean of the Viterbi School a decade ago, Nikias allocated $160,000 to fund a student group that aspired to create the first entirely student designed and built rocket to reach space and safely return. In 2006, the newly created Rocket Propulsion Lab launched its first effort, dubbed Del Carbon, which reached a maximum altitude of 21,500 feet and speeds of up to Mach 1.4.

By 2015, the lab was refining a Del Carbon Extreme, setting its sights on reaching more than 10 times the altitude of the original rocket and four times the speed. USC's faculty, recognizing the ability of such projects to give invaluable experience to students in the job market, have worked to coordinate and expand these programs through the Space Engineering Research Center and related efforts.

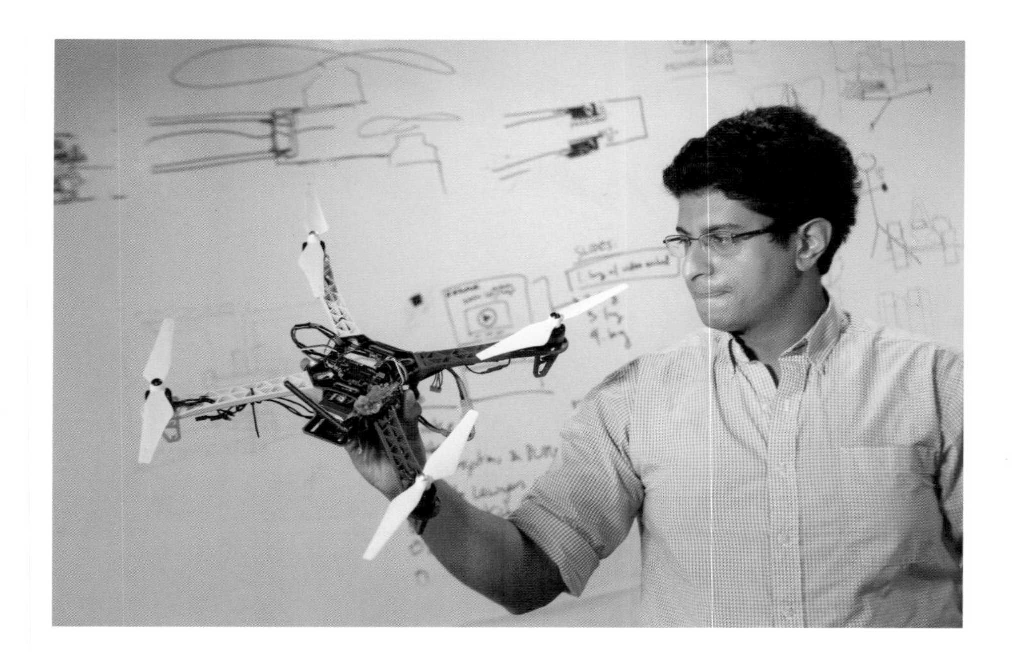

The Viterbi Startup Garage is a venture incubation program that nurtures emerging businesses. The program, launched in 2013, offers students and alumni a combination of funding and guidance from the USC Viterbi School of Engineering.

A Research University in Blossom

In his 2014 annual presidential address to the faculty, Nikias praised their ability to compete for a piece of a shrinking funding pie. "Nationally, there has not been a tougher funding climate in our lifetimes," Nikias said. "Still, funding for USC research is at an all-time high. Over the previous year, total federal expenditures once again topped $450 million, and total research expenditures topped $600 million again." He also cited the university's strategic recruiting of superstar faculty as having a galvanizing effect, injecting more than $120 million in high-profile research grants over the previous three years alone.

Ultimately, though, the goal at USC wasn't to approach the wonder of discovery in conventional ways, or to measure it according to the usual metrics. As Nikias noted in his 2009 Pullias Lecture, delivered while he was provost, "the future cannot be micromanaged." As he put it:

> Even the best efforts to predict the future fall short of the best efforts of the human imagination in action. The future is generally more peculiar, and more wonderful, and more textured, than we could have imagined. We need not predict the future with great certainty; rather, we need to create a dynamic environment in which we can react and change rapidly.

At USC, that dynamic environment was just beginning to emerge.

Army-funded research efforts at USC explore the use of camera-enabled quadrotors, drones, and other robotic technologies.

Chapter 6

Storming the Frontiers of Health and Medicine

USC's Medical Enterprise Charges Forward

When C. L. Max Nikias delivered his first formal address as president, on August 25, 2010, the venue was USC's Health Sciences Campus, before hundreds of assembled faculty and staff. The setting was not incidental. USC's leadership had chosen that location in order to make a point indisputably clear: Health and medicine would take center stage in the life of the great universities of the 21st century, and USC would adjust its financial priorities accordingly. The purchase of two hospitals from Tenet Healthcare in 2009 represented something of a down payment on that investment, Nikias said in his address.

"Given USC's location and our international heritage and our academic strengths," Nikias told the audience, "this university can hope to embody the intersection of the Pacific century and the biological century. This is an unimaginable opportunity, in which we can help shape the very fabric of this age."

Repositioning the University to Serve a New Queen

What was the urgency attached to this shift in focus? Nikias had come to USC as a renowned expert in digital signal processing and a passionate champion of the Greco-Roman classical canon. Lesser known was his background at the intersection of biomedicine and technology. That expertise proved providential as the university's leaders began to consider how much it should invest in its medical and healthcare enterprise.

Academic headwinds were moving in a medically oriented direction, and at first glance this trend did not seem favorable to USC's ambitious goals of increasing its influence and impact. As Nikias explained to the academic community, the university had ridden in the forefront of various revolutions over the past 130 years—including those in aerospace, digital media, and wireless communications. But the next revolution was poised to happen at the frontiers

The plaza of USC's medical center proudly displays its new name. The W. M. Keck Foundation pledged a historic $150 million naming gift in 2011 to accelerate innovations in medical, clinical, and translational research and education. This was the foundation's second nine-figure gift to advance the health sciences at USC; the first was a $110 million donation in 1999. In recognition, the university renamed its medical enterprise Keck Medicine of USC in perpetuity.

of biology and medicine. Just as top research institutions of the past half century were home to the best engineering schools, the leaders of the future would be those with the best medical centers. And in this area, USC needed to make up academic ground quickly or risk becoming marginalized.

While USC had a solid, respected healthcare enterprise, its faculty had few of the advantages of their peers at other leading institutions, in terms of conducting research, offering education, and delivering services. At some point, the university would have to make a decision: Would it be content to be

USC celebrates the Keck Foundation's gift in 2011. At the event are (from left): then-Provost Elizabeth Garrett; Edward P. Roski Jr., then chair of the Board of Trustees; Keck Foundation chair Robert A. Day; and President Nikias.

The Keck Foundation's $150 million naming gift, along with enabling a host of academic and infrastructure improvements to USC's Health Sciences Campus, represented a major milestone in the university's quest to become the premier healthcare destination for patients across Southern California and around the Pacific Rim.

a minor player in healthcare and instead build on its other existing strengths, such as digital media, informatics, and the arts? Or would it make a risky gamble to increase its positioning in health and medicine—and commit to the corresponding investments?

In his 2010 address on the Health Sciences Campus, Nikias spoke in terms of the USC academic community recognizing a "new queen" in the royal court of higher education:

> The queen of the sciences in the 20th century was physics—and, as a result, electronics. At USC, we believe electronics will continue to be important. But she will give up her crown to another queen in the 21st century.
>
> The very laws of physics limit the growth of conventional electronics. But because of electronics, forces are gathering in such a way that this century is poised to be the age of medicine and biology. We can hope for breakthroughs in these areas—which will open up entire new sectors of the global economy. It is here that we will see the fastest-growing industries of this century. New technology can reshape medicine with applications in drug delivery and patient care. We can see new therapeutic products

The recruitment of Andrew P. McMahon from Harvard University was a major boost for the Eli and Edythe Broad Center for Regenerative Medicine and Stem Cell Research at USC. At a ceremony honoring his arrival are (from left): Keck School dean Carmen Puliafito; President Nikias; key benefactor Eli Broad; and Professor McMahon.

The Eli and Edythe Broad Center for Regenerative Medicine and Stem Cell Research opened its doors in the fall of 2010. Partnering with the California Institute for Regenerative Medicine, USC has been able to, in the words of Professor Andrew McMahon, build "powerful, cross-institutional teams that have united research around the goals of regenerative medicine to treat a host of diseases affecting humanity."

> unlike anything to date. And we can see new ideas move from the bench to the bedside—faster and more intelligently than ever.

USC's leadership also pointed to other realities, including population trends, the passage of the Affordable Care Act (and the resulting shuffle and expansion of American citizens' medical coverage), and the limited latitude of budget-strapped public universities to meet emerging needs.

While many premier academic medical centers found it difficult to move in new directions, USC was able to pivot toward whatever emerging pathways were most promising. The recession of 2008 had put many universities in a position in which they had to borrow simply to meet payroll, while USC—by contrast a fiscally prudent institution—had stockpiled $500 million in working capital.

That cash reserve allowed the university to take the first major step in its reinvention as a powerhouse in health and medicine, through the purchase of USC University Hospital and USC Norris Cancer Hospital in 2009. These acquisitions would pave the way for the institution to build a medical enterprise that could integrate research, education, and patient care on its own ambitious terms.

In an instant, the portion of the overall budget dedicated to medical endeavors had rocketed from 14 percent to 45 percent. "Overnight, USC had become a different kind of animal," Nikias observed.

Next came a coordinated effort to incorporate the two vast healthcare organizations quickly and smoothly into the fiber of the larger university. Within less than a year, USC had successfully integrated all 19 faculty practice plans at the two hospitals, along with 520 clinical doctors. Nikias would later say that Senior Vice President Tom Jackiewicz, Keck School dean Carmen Puliafito, and then-Provost Elizabeth Garrett had brought "energy, wisdom, and persistence to this astonishing metamorphosis."

In another major upgrade of its clinical efforts, USC broke ground in 2013 on the Norris Healthcare Consultation Center. From left: President Nikias; Harlyne J. Norris, a trustee of both USC and the Norris Foundation; Lisa Hansen, chair of the board of trustees for the Norris Foundation; and Tom Jackiewicz, senior vice president at USC.

Examining a Rapid March Forward

In October 2014, President Nikias reconvened the Health Sciences Campus community to revisit the goals the university had set out four years earlier and to take measure of recent progress and future challenges.

The university's medical ambitions required money. He reported that USC had by that point already raised $3.7 billion of its historic $6 billion goal in the *Fas Regna Trojae* campaign—and that a third of that funding was dedicated to medicine, the biological sciences, and health professions. Included in that amount were several major endorsements of USC's efforts:

- A $150 million gift from the Keck Foundation in 2011 (in addition to its landmark $110 million gift in 1999) to support and name the entire medical enterprise;
- A $50 million gift from Trustee Ming Hsieh to spark innovation across medicine and engineering, including the dramatic emerging realm of nanotechnology;
- A $50 million gift from the renowned spinal surgeon Gary K. Michelson to establish the USC Michelson Center for Convergent Bioscience, paving the way for breakthroughs at the crossroads of science and technology;
- And more than 1,200 donations from grateful patients who now considered themselves full and committed members of the Trojan Family.

To accomplish its goals, a leading medical enterprise would require an undisputed reputation for excellence along prominent frontiers. For USC, this meant bringing in outside partners in research and education, a strategy in line with

The Norris Healthcare Consultation Center was taking shape in the fall of 2015, with completion scheduled for the following year. The building was made possible by a lead gift from the Kenneth T. and Eileen L. Norris Foundation.

the larger, university-wide priority of establishing a critical mass of outstanding faculty who would draw attention and funding. In pursuit of this ambitious objective, Nikias later said, "We aimed for the stars—and we reached them."

The recruitment efforts yielded a new generation of medical leadership, including 12 new faculty chairs in the Keck School of Medicine and six new directors of research centers and institutes. Since the acquisition of the two hospitals in 2009, USC has brought more than 70 major faculty recruits to the Keck School, including world-renowned talent from Caltech, the Cleveland Clinic, Johns Hopkins, Stanford, Cedars-Sinai Medical Center, University of Michigan, UCSF, UCLA, Vanderbilt, and Northwestern.

Outside observers marveled at how some of the world's top researchers in health and medicine were streaming into USC from institutions that were more established in those fields. In key emerging disciplines like neuroscience, the university was becoming what Nikias called an "intellectual magnet."

Among the recruits were several elite research groups, ranging from a dozen to more than a hundred strong. One triumph that drew considerable attention in the scientific and higher education communities came in 2013, when the brain-science researchers Arthur Toga and Paul Thompson moved their globally renowned Laboratory of Neuro Imaging from UCLA to USC—with a complement of 110 faculty, researchers, and graduate students.

The pattern was repeated the next year, when internationally famous pioneers in molecular biology Raymond Stevens and Peter Kuhn left the

prestigious Scripps Research Institute in the San Diego area and relocated to USC. They brought with them an acclaimed, 50-person research team. Like biomedical engineer Scott Fraser, who came from Caltech, and stem-cell expert Andrew P. McMahon, who moved from Harvard, these researchers were drawn to the USC approach, which was more entrepreneurial and flexible than those of most other institutions, and they believed it would enable them to make more rapid academic progress.

As with many of USC's high-profile hires, these teams were brought in to accelerate progress at the intersection of a number of key academic disciplines.

Between 2010 and 2015, the university rapidly and dramatically expanded its healthcare footprint across Southern California by opening new offices and establishing partnerships. The Beverly Hills location of Keck Medicine of USC opened its doors in 2011.

Carol Mauch Amir, senior vice president of the university, has been instrumental in coordinating the expansion and integration of USC's academic medical center.

The recruits represented new partnerships for the university's current faculty, bringing with them fresh perspectives and ideas—along with a whopping $140 million in funding from the National Institutes of Health.

"These were shots heard around the country and around the world," Nikias would tell the Health Sciences Campus community in his 2014 address. "These showed that we have reached the point where, finally, we can recruit anyone we want. Not just excellent talent, but rare, better-than-excellent talent, game-changing talent, and we will continue to do so."

The university achieved many academic victories during these important transitional years. A host of USC schools, institutes, and centers for medicine, life sciences, engineering, pharmacy, and dentistry together made an extraordinary commitment to convergent bioscience. They paved the way for Gary Michelson's $50 million gift in January 2014 to create the USC Michelson Center for Convergent Bioscience.

Children's Hospital Los Angeles, often mentioned as USC's "third campus," strengthened its position as a top-five leader nationally and also bolstered its work in key areas including personalized medicine. The university and CHLA recruited a number of new stars, and established the Institute for the Developing Mind and the Translational Biomedical Imaging Laboratory.

President Nikias, Trustee Mark Stevens, and his wife, Mary, participate in an October 2015 ceremony honoring their $50 million gift to name the USC Mark and Mary Stevens Neuroimaging and Informatics Institute. Seated on the left are institute heads Arthur Toga and Paul Thompson and Keck School dean Carmen Puliafito.

The university community celebrates USC's acquisition of the Verdugo Hills Hospital in 2013. The healthcare facility provides faculty and clinicians with an important base from which to serve the San Gabriel Valley area.

And in 2015, Toga and Thompson's institute received a major boost when benefactors Mark Stevens and his wife, Mary, donated $50 million to endow it as the USC Mark and Mary Stevens Neuroimaging and Informatics Institute. The funding would advance the research collective's work in treating and preventing brain injury and disease, including Alzheimer's, schizophrenia, and related ailments.

A Distinct Leadership Role for a Private Academic Medical Enterprise

Characteristically, when Nikias delivered his 2014 special address, the mood wasn't one of complacent satisfaction with the university's progress in the health sciences. Rather, it was one of determination—to raise the bar (and the stakes) still higher. Could USC truly move past the entrenched old guard, and build an academic medical enterprise that would provide direction and inspiration to its elite peers? In his speech to the Trojan healthcare community, Nikias offered four reasons it could do just that.

First, he noted that USC's status as a fully private independent university with a long entrepreneurial streak gave it a particular nimbleness. It could quickly move in new directions along emerging frontiers in a way that its

bureaucracy-burdened competitors could only envy.

Second, he noted that medical innovation would necessarily be across multiple fields, and that USC is "uniquely broad and interdisciplinary" in ways that others aspire to but could not easily achieve.

Third, he returned to the idea that USC stood at a providential intersection of time and place. "This is indeed the century of the Pacific, and this is the century of the human health revolution," Nikias said. "Our university stands at the nexus of both of these, here in the Los Angeles basin, this amazing, 14-million-people-strong microcosm of our new world." Southern California, he said, was the "greatest living laboratory for the health challenges of the 21st century," and the university needed to be in a position to make full use of that vast resource.

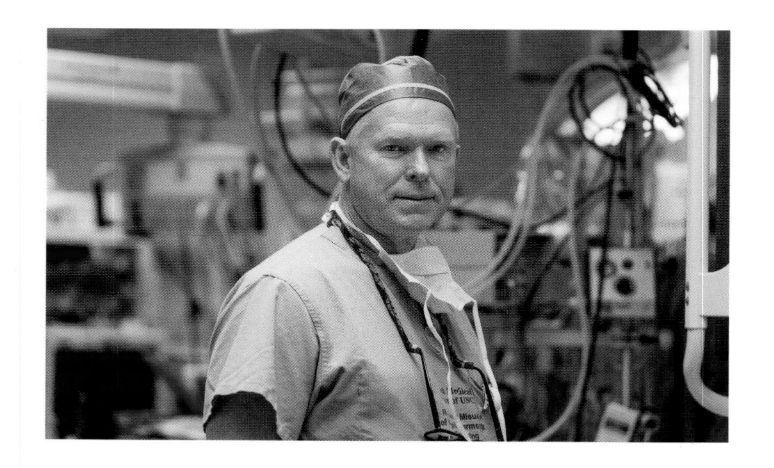

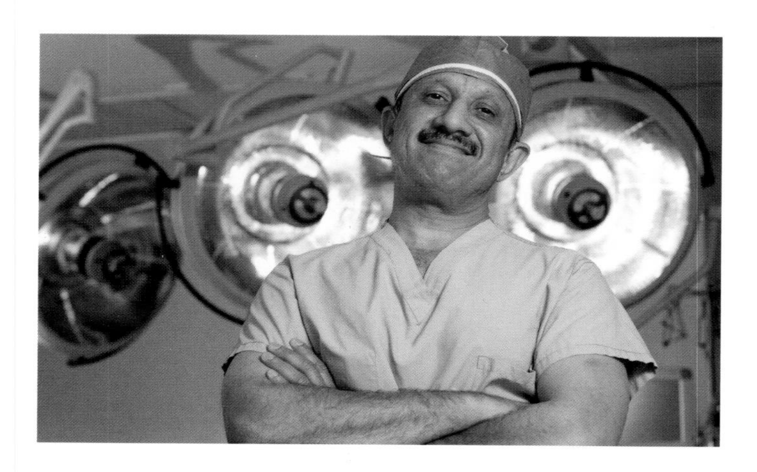

Nikias, noting that USC was one of only two large private American research universities west of Chicago, suggested to the Trojan community that it had an opportunity—even a "duty"—to shape the future of global healthcare. "All of the other 25 private competitors of ours are east of Chicago," he said, observing that this gave them latitude to lead. "After 135 years since our founding," he told faculty, "finally our geographic location works to our advantage" in a world now tilting toward the Pacific.

And fourth, he argued that even though USC was proudly private and independent, it was in the school's DNA to achieve a level of service that exceeded that of any private university, and more than perhaps any public research institution. This commitment included service to the local community; to the Los Angeles County+USC Medical Center; to its partner, Children's Hospital Los Angeles; and increasingly, to citizens on a global scale, at a moment when the Trojan Family was now 350,000 strong across all continents.

Nikias went on to reaffirm a goal he had announced at the outset of his presidency: that the university should seek to establish the premier academic medical center for the Pacific Rim. While that overall objective may have seemed lofty and almost vague, he proposed a key benchmark along the way that was both tangible and formidable: The university should, he said, claim Southern California for itself and be satisfied with nothing less than being the single market leader in regional healthcare.

USC's reputation in the health sciences received a boost from the work of its star faculty. Clockwise from top left: Vaughn Starnes is chair of the department of cardiothoracic surgery and director of the USC Cardiovascular Thoracic Institute; Rohit Varma serves as chair of the department of ophthalmology and director of the USC Gayle and Edward Roski Eye Institute; and Inderbir S. Gill is associate dean for clinical innovation at the Keck School and founding executive director of the USC Institute of Urology.

Given the dominance of more established rivals in this arena, Nikias acknowledged the odds could seem insurmountable. But he pointed again to USC's recent progress in medicine—the swift expansion of its healthcare footprint, the dramatic rise in revenue, and the recruiting of the world's best faculty in major medical specialties—as well as the restrictions facing the university's competitors, and suggested that it was time to press on for maximum advantage.

USC needed to grow the Keck medical enterprise in size and academic quality "by every means available," he said. This would be achieved through recruiting more top-notch faculty in both basic sciences and clinical programs; new alliances and partnerships with research institutes, hospitals, and physician groups; strategic acquisitions; and expanding research collaborations between medical and biological sciences, engineering, and the health professions.

Nikias then announced a plan to double the size of USC's physician network to more than 1,200 clinical doctors and expand the university health system's footprint to triple its current size, "while ensuring that patient safety and experience always remain in the forefront, never to be compromised."

He concluded that USC needed to seize a moment in which ongoing market consolidation in healthcare—and the expansion of coverage to 9 million more Californians—could allow the university to set a new standard.

USC's Clinical Care Enterprise Comes of Age

USC's progress in research and education had be married to the best work in clinical care, in order to establish true leadership in medicine and achieve the goals that had been set out by the president. The university needed to make fast progress along that front, and by 2015 several statistics showed that those advances were quickly being made:

- USC's hospital earnings had grown from being in the red to $50 million.
- Most of the clinical service lines at the Keck Medical Center (including urology, cancer, cardiovascular, neurosciences, and spine, among others) were two years ahead of their targets.
- Inpatient discharges had grown by more than 30 percent, even as state-wide discharges had contracted by 7 percent.

W. M. Keck Foundation chair Robert A. Day and President Nikias celebrate the announcement of the Keck Foundation's landmark naming gift to USC's medical enterprise.

- Keck Medicine's total revenue had increased by 150 percent, to $1.2 billion by the fall of 2014. (Prior to the purchase of the two hospitals, it had never exceeded $390 million.)

USC was also making dramatic gains in patient safety grades and acuity rates, a measurement that represents the difficulty of cases handled. The university's clinical faculty showed the highest acuity rate west of the Mississippi, a telling indicator of its ability to treat the most high-risk patients.

During these years, USC established new partners in clinical care, strategically expanding its healthcare footprint across Southern California. It acquired and integrated the Verdugo Hills Hospital in the La Cañada/Glendale area, as well as a premier oncology and hematology group in Orange County. USC and Keck also created a presence across Beverly Hills, downtown Los Angeles, the South Bay, and Pasadena, and expanded services on the University Park Campus.

The burgeoning of excellence was mirrored in physical improvements and beautification under way throughout the Health Sciences Campus. A 120,000-square-foot building on Soto Street opened in 2011, offering crucial additional space to house the Keck School of Medicine's department of preventive medicine—as well as laboratories, classrooms, administrative offices, and a café and fitness center for students and faculty. USC also began construction on a top-flight 200-room hotel; and the entire campus received a makeover to match the beloved architectural signature of the core of the University Park Campus.

Making Southern California a Global Biotechnology Hub

In his 2014 address, Nikias announced that USC would be "relentless in working with the county and the city to establish a biotech park on the Health Sciences Campus where the county yards are currently located."

USC's efforts in healthcare extend beyond its campuses and satellite locations, drawing together a range of partners in academia, industry, and government to help establish Los Angeles as a leading hub of the biomedical revolution.

The new name in world-class medicine.
Keck Medical Center of USC
Fight On.
Keck Medical Center

A constellation of faculty stars is bringing attention to USC's medical enterprise. Clockwise from top left: Jay Lieberman, chair of the Department of Orthopaedic Surgery; Larissa Rodríguez, professor of urology and director of USC Female Pelvic Medicine and Reconstructive Surgery; and John Niparko, chair of the Caruso Department of Otolaryngology-Head and Neck Surgery.

By late February 2015, the president and USC had already managed to convene a regional summit to begin the endeavor of creating a local biotechnology ecosystem that would generate new businesses and jobs, attract venture capital, and spark tangible forms of innovation in health and medicine. Los Angeles City Council members and officials, along with representatives of other academic and medical institutions, gathered to discuss how best to expedite the building of a park that could accomplish such goals and turn the region into a true global hub of the still-nascent health revolution.

In a *Los Angeles Times* op-ed in February 2015, Nikias argued that Southern California could play a primary rather than secondary role in this important field:

> California is home to two major biotechnology hubs—San Francisco and San Diego—but Los Angeles has been left behind. The paradox is that universities in Los Angeles County produce more than 5,000 graduates in biotechnology-related fields each year, compared with 2,800 in San Francisco-Oakland-Fremont. However, it's San Francisco that attracted $1.15 billion in biotechnology investment in 2013, compared with a paltry $45 million here. No wonder, then, that so many of our graduates head north.
>
> To reverse this trend, Los Angeles requires an ecosystem that fosters business, venture capital investment, and access to academic medical centers for research and clinical trials. My university, USC, hopes to spark this change by building a Biotechnology Park adjacent to our Health Sciences Campus in Boyle Heights.
>
> With the cooperation of Caltech, community colleges, the L.A. Unified School District, and other institutions, this will represent the first step in a plan for a robust biotechnology corridor in the surrounding area. The corridor will provide space for established companies, training for entry-level jobs, and incubators for start-up firms.
>
> Pharmaceutical, biotechnology, and biomedical companies have already expressed interest. Such companies rely on university partners for research and development, and our Biotechnology Park would give them the infrastructure to flourish.

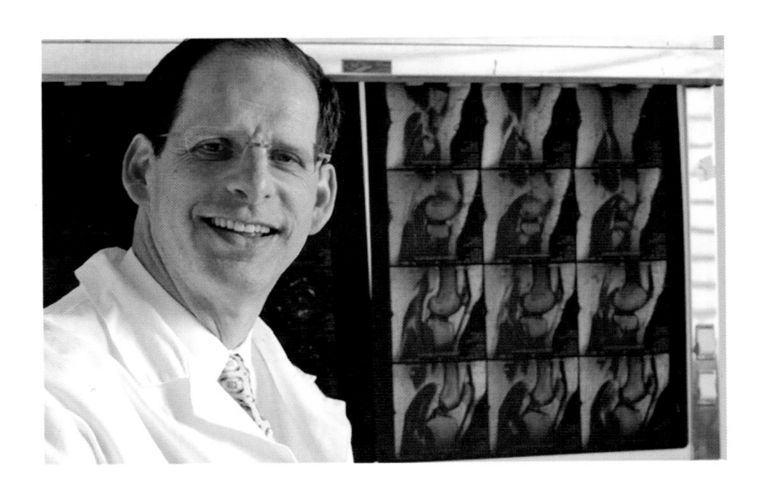

All of the ingredients for Los Angeles to capture growth in this booming field are already here. With the right alignment between government, academia, and industry, we can harness the region's existing strengths—including our science graduates—to create lasting economic growth.

On the March

Nikias, known as a Greek classicist, harked back in his 2014 address to an ancient tale of beating the odds to reaffirm USC's ambitious healthcare goals. The story involved how the troops of a Greek general, Epaminondas, had managed to turn long-standing history on its head by boldly taking on a challenge that others shrank from. Said Nikias:

> There is a story from antiquity that seems relevant to where we are today, and where we aspire to go next. Go back some 2,400 years to when the men and women of Thebes were in conflict with Sparta. In 371 BC, the Spartan army invaded Boeotia, and they were close to taking over Thebes. The entire Greek world of antiquity had feared Sparta. No one dared take them head-on. But a Theban general by the name of Epaminondas and his army faced down the Spartans at Leuctra, even though they were outnumbered two to one.

The Thebans crushed the Spartan army. Suddenly the Spartan aura of invincibility evaporated. Suddenly their expanding empire was vulnerable. But it wasn't enough for the Thebans to simply protect their own turf. Eighteen months later, General Epaminondas surprised the ancient Greek world again by rejecting conventional military tactics. For 400 years, no army had ever dared to cross the Isthmus of Corinth and march south toward Sparta.

So, against all expectations, Epaminondas and his troops marched south during wintertime. In that era, conventional wisdom held that you simply don't attempt that kind of attack during the winter. But the Thebans were determined. They marched 200 miles, through the bitter cold and rain. They crossed the isthmus, then moved confidently into the den of the Spartan lion, in Laconia. As a result, the Thebans not only pushed over the

The Soto Building on USC's Health Sciences Campus opened in 2011. The three-story, mixed-use building houses administrative and academic units, classrooms, a café, and a 10,000-square-foot fitness center.

Construction on the Malcolm and Barbara Currie Residence Hall began in 2014, with a target completion date of 2016. Currie Hall represents a milestone in the establishment of a residential learning community on USC's Health Sciences Campus.

> invincible Spartans; they humiliated them. They shook Spartan dominance to its core. The Thebans reshaped the 400-year political map of Greece in just two years.

Nikias suggested that in the healthcare arena, USC need not fear any invincible, older rivals as long as its academic community remained bold enough to march into the heart of the challenge. After all, its recent victories were a foretaste of the "sort of reshaping of the medical sciences and healthcare map of Southern California that you have been doing in just the past four years. The aura of invincibility of other medical centers in the region evaporated because of you." With that, he asked the faculty to "pledge together today to keep reshaping it in the future."

Reaction to the president's charge was enthusiastic and emphatic, both in the academic and broader communities. A *Los Angeles Magazine* feature on Nikias acknowledged how "USC has strengthened its 'brand' in healthcare." And new and existing faculty moved forward with creative health-related endeavors spanning the university's various campuses and research centers.

By the fall of 2015, USC had made rapid gains across Southern California, spanning from Orange County to northern Los Angeles. Epaminondas's troops were on the march.

Students in USC's School of Cinematic Arts and School of Dramatic Arts work together to create a video celebrating the launch of the USC Kaufman School of Dance. The new school was established by Glorya Kaufman, a noted philanthropist and champion of the performing arts.

Chapter 7

USC's Secret Weapon

Arts Programs Enjoy a New Spotlight

The past century of technological and scientific progress has had a profound impact on how society, and its research universities, have viewed priorities in education. At many institutions, the arts and humanities seemed to lack the attention, energy, and resources that were being invested in the fast-growing scientific and technological fields. In recent years, as policy makers and journalists worried about the United States losing its edge in "STEM" (science, technology, engineering, and math) education, the cultural and artistic pursuits were gradually pushed even further from center stage.

USC, however, had been following a different script, thanks in large part to its long-established, renowned schools in the arts: the USC Roski School of Art and Design, the USC School of Architecture, the USC School of Cinematic Arts, the USC School of Dramatic Arts, and the USC Thornton School of Music. Within these freestanding, independent schools, USC's arts programs enjoyed autonomy and respect rare for these disciplines at top research universities.

The term "interdisciplinarity" has been for several years a buzzword in higher education. Interdisciplinarity encourages experts from different fields to collaborate, so that in the process they might see problems from fresh perspectives and find creative solutions. As the concept of innovation also became a priority in larger society, universities recognized that new ideas are spawned most fruitfully at the intersection of different disciplines—between biology and engineering, for example, or between digital media and the arts.

But it is easier to talk about the importance of interdisciplinarity than to achieve it in a meaningful form. In its arts programs, USC houses a large engine of creative energy and a culture of experimentation and risk-taking. Often out of necessity, it developed an atmosphere of cooperation and collaboration among its vast array of independent schools. By contrast, faculty at other universities have tended to work out of "silos," or fiefdoms, jealously protecting their turf and funding, and sometimes seeing potential collaborators as rivals.

USC was seeking to make more than a decade's worth of academic progress in just a few years at this crucial moment in time. As provost and later as president, Nikias would often describe the arts at USC as "our secret weapon." These programs, and their talented faculty and students, infused the larger academic community with imagination and a spirit of unlimited possibility, he said. In turn, students and faculty in the arts gained from access to many of the best minds in emerging technology, the sciences, social sciences, and the professions.

Infusing Creative Energy into an Entire Campus

The ongoing development of the arts and humanities at USC has reflected a key academic commitment of President Nikias, even as more research-driven disciplines increasingly dominated the higher education landscape in the United States, and more so in emerging economies such as China and India.

Nikias is certainly himself a technologist: winner of the IEEE Simon Ramo Medal, member of the National Academy of Engineering, and architect of USC's vaunted national multimedia research center (the Integrated Media Systems Center).

But he is also equal parts a humanist, and in fact was the inaugural holder of the Malcolm R. Currie Chair in Technology and the Humanities, established by the technology legend and former chair of USC's Board of Trustees. Nikias's particular expertise focuses on Greek history, literature, and theater, but he believes that for students to be properly educated and for society to prosper, the full array of the arts needs to be nurtured. "Science and technology are means toward an end," he wrote in the *San Francisco Chronicle*. "But art is our true end as fully mature human beings living in society."

Nikias's passion for the arts was such that, beginning when he was provost, he set aside time to lead seminars for incoming freshmen on the rise of Athenian democracy and drama. These intimate gatherings of 10 to 15 students were in many cases their first personal interaction with any member of the USC faculty. Since becoming president, Nikias has continued to teach these seminars, in order to give undergraduates important historical context to the cultural opportunities and experiences they will encounter at USC in their next few years.

Illustrious musician, conductor, and USC alumnus Michael Tilson Thomas leads the university's Thornton Symphony, one of the world's finest collegiate ensembles. Tilson Thomas joined the faculty in 2015 as a Judge Widney Professor.

The establishment of Visions & Voices: The Arts and Humanities Initiative in 2006 also provided substantial momentum for the arts. In announcing the program—created to leverage those studies to full educational effect across the university community—Nikias stated that the goal "is not merely to entertain audiences but to challenge them at the core of their being." Through this series of performances, lectures, and other events programmed to include an intentional reflective component, students from every field are able to gain creative insights, a timeless understanding of human nature, and an appreciation of USC's essential academic values.

The Visions & Voices program quickly became a standing-room-only success. Students continue to line up, sometimes for hours, for prime seats

The USC Kaufman School of Dance, established with the extraordinary support of philanthropist Glorya Kaufman in 2012, welcomed its first class in 2015. The Kaufman School, with the accomplished dance-world veteran and educator Jodie Gates (at center) serving as its inaugural director and vice dean, represents the university's sixth independent arts school.

at events on campus and in Los Angeles's bustling cultural hot spots. Over the course of an academic year, the series typically draws more than 25,000 attendees through a rich offering of nearly a hundred programs and events.

A Vibrant Arts Curriculum

By 2015, USC had 6,000 students majoring or minoring in its arts schools, perhaps the largest such contingent at any research university. These students and their faculty alone would constitute one of the largest institutions for the creative and performing arts in the world. But rather than pursuing their individual artistic disciplines in isolation, they worked in harmony with experts across diverse fields.

As the university continued to grow as a research powerhouse, its core academic arts programs—in addition to being distinguished in their own right—increasingly gave USC faculty a strategic edge in the sciences, technology, and professions. Experts in engineering or medicine, for example, could work with experts in cinematic arts or theater to develop unique ways to monitor progress, communicate information, and deliver education.

For USC to fully exploit its secret academic weapon, it would need to invest in both strengthening its existing academic programs and developing new ones. Through a combination of high-level endowments and an overall commitment to innovations in the university's current programs, the stage was set for a renewed era of artistic progress.

Creative Movement: Dance Comes to Center Stage

In 2012, philanthropist Glorya Kaufman pledged the largest gift in the history of American dance to establish an unprecedented sixth independent arts school at USC. At this point in its metamorphosis, the university saw the opportunity to expand the breadth of its offerings—but there was no room for

The USC School of Cinematic Arts today offers enviable technologies to train the next generation of storytellers. Cutting-edge facilities, such as the Interactive Media Building (above), were strategically designed to maximize students' and faculty members' ability to explore and collaborate with new media forms.

error in terms of quality. Any new school needed to be exceptional from the outset. Kaufman's vision and gift made this possible.

The university broke ground on the school's home in 2014, with plans to create a facility that would nurture the evolution of the venerable art. "A world-class school needs a world-class building," said Robert Cutietta, concurrently dean of the USC Thornton School of Music and the founding dean of the dance school, at the groundbreaking of the Glorya Kaufman International Dance Center. "Thanks to Ms. Kaufman's generosity, we'll have both. I can't wait to welcome our first students to this magnificent building." The 55,000-foot facility will include spaces for studio performance, five medium and small dance studios, a dance wellness center, dressing rooms, classrooms and offices for faculty and staff, and a large collaborative area for students.

The school received more than 370 applications for only 25 seats in its first freshman class, in 2015, for a selectivity rate of under 7 percent. The program also attracted outstanding faculty, including the acclaimed choreographer William Forsythe.

Miracles in the Garage

In the spring of 2014, one of USC's newest independent interdisciplinary programs sent out acceptance letters to its first class of students. And the unconventional manner in which it did so said much about its mission.

Many of the world's greatest technological advances have blossomed in humble garages. The innovative USC Iovine and Young Academy features its own creative space, "The Garage," where talented interdisciplinary students are able to work on new pathways and breakthroughs.

Applicants to the USC Jimmy Iovine and Andre Young Academy for Arts, Technology and the Business of Innovation needed to demonstrate the breadth of their interests and skills and succinctly express a compelling vision for tackling challenges. Each of the 31 individuals who made the cut received a personalized video from the school's founders, with the two music-industry icons warmly welcoming them into the program by name and wishing them a bright future.

Established by a historic $70 million gift from Jimmy Iovine and Andre "Dr. Dre" Young in 2013, the program would immerse broadly talented students in the invigorating waters of the arts, sciences, and social sciences, in an environment designed to help them invent the future. On campus the facility became known as "The Garage."

The founders have described its mission as nothing less than to unleash a wave of talent like that of legendary Apple CEO Steve Jobs. They believed that the right atmosphere could summon forth such world-shaping, game-changing innovators on a regular basis. And they were convinced that USC was the place where such an investment would bear the most fruit. It served as a powerful validation of the university's "secret weapon," which was now becoming far less of a secret.

"The academy's core education will create a common, multilingual literacy and fluency across essential disciplines," said Erica Muhl, inaugural director of the program. "This 'big picture' knowledge and skill will equip graduates with a

President Nikias is an engineer by training but also a classicist and an advocate for the arts. Each fall, he leads entering freshmen on a two-day journey through the themes and development of ancient Athenian drama.

leadership perspective that is unparalleled in an undergraduate degree, and that will be applicable to virtually any industry."

Innovations in Existing Arts Programs

Throughout USC's arts enterprises, innovation has flourished. In addition to her role at the academy, Muhl has also served as dean of the USC Roski School of Fine Arts since 2012. In late 2013, the latter changed its name to the USC Roski School of Art and Design, in recognition of a broader mission that integrated it into the larger academic life of the university. "The new name represents a subtle yet momentous shift in how our students identify themselves and their work within contemporary visual culture," Muhl said. This shift meant additions to the program at a practical level—such as a graphic design course in fashion marketing and a new minor in 3-D design—and a greater connection to the collective conversation about art and design in society at large.

The USC School of Architecture has become a more global school than many of its peers, as symbolized by its accomplished dean, Qingyun Ma, who bridges Shanghai and Los Angeles in his professional and academic practices. In 2011, President Nikias appointed the school's acclaimed graduate Frank Gehry to the USC faculty; the designer of some of the world's most iconic structures now serves as a Judge Widney Professor of Architecture.

The USC School of Cinematic Arts, bolstered by a $175 million gift from famed alumnus George Lucas a few years earlier, has developed the most sophisticated infrastructure of any contemporary film school. The improvements allow it to play an influential role in the emerging mega-industry of video game design, as well as immersive and virtual reality breakthroughs in education and in training for the military. The third and final phase of construction for the school's new facility, completed in 2013, made room to house its Interactive Media & Games Division, the Media Arts+Practice Division,

RIGHT: USC welcomed its inaugural class of International Artist Fellows in 2013. From left: Jacinto Astiazarán, a Mexican filmmaker; Vladimir Gorbach, a classical guitarist from Russia; Fei Kayser, a Chinese playwright; and Frederico Fernandez, a visual artist from Brazil.

and the leading-edge R+D labs, which focus on rapidly developing areas such as virtual, alternate, and mixed reality experiences.

International Artist Fellowship Program

USC also strengthened and leveraged its arts programs by creating additional educational opportunities at the graduate level. In 2013, the university launched the International Artist Fellowship Program, fulfilling one of the commitments Nikias had made in his 2010 inaugural speech. In that address, he proclaimed:

> Let the best young minds from across the Pacific Rim compete to receive a USC education. Let us build special scholarship programs for students represented from all Pacific Rim nations. Let them take full advantage of a highly diverse environment they won't find anywhere else.
>
> Great talent exists in America and around the Pacific Rim. Let that talent be refined in the unique intellectual crucible here, which represents a dynamic blend of the arts and humanities and culture, and cutting-edge science and technology, and social sciences and professions.

The program identifies some of the most brilliant young artistic talents, particularly from around the Pacific Rim and Latin America, and brings them to campus, where they have the funding and support necessary to experiment freely in building bridges between the arts and other fields.

The initial class attracted fellows from several nations and continents. Jacinto Astiazarán, a Tijuana native and Mexico City resident whose work has been exhibited internationally, came to further develop his skills in the use of video, dance, and other forms of performance to depict the process of cultural adaptation. Fei Kayser, a playwright from China, said she hoped to grow in

LEFT: Michael Chang, a student at the USC Roski School of Art and Design, works on an intricate watercolor painting. The oldest art institute in Southern California, the school opened its doors in 1883.

Students in the School of Dramatic Arts perform a crowd-pleasing production of the musical *Grease*. The school typically stages more than 20 shows annually.

Each year, Visions & Voices begins its season with a dynamic multimedia spectacle, often featuring performances from pop musicians, spoken-word artists, and street dance troupes, such as We Are Heroes, who performed at the first kickoff event, in 2011.

her ability to author plays that capture the multilayered nature of life in her homeland. Vladimir Gorbach, a classical musician from Russia, described his guitar as "kind of a lonely instrument," to which his fellowship would offer a remedy, enabling him to connect to L.A.'s active chamber music scene. And Frederico Fernandez, a Brazilian street artist, arrived with the goal of making animated films, courtesy of the vanguard technical resources in the university's arts complex.

A Game Changer

A recurring theme in the USC story is that—although it may have lacked certain resources of other leading universities—it continually moved forward by making shrewd and mindful use of its distinct and unique advantages.

For years, USC had a far higher number of independent professional schools than rival universities—a natural result of its founding mission to educate a complete range of professionals for a fast-growing region. Some observers felt this was a handicap for USC, as it was spread across too many areas, diminishing its potential to develop any one "elite" program.

Yet as the focus in higher education has shifted in the past two decades from hyper-specialization to broad and collaborative interdisciplinarity, USC's

seeming weakness has become a strength. And this strength has been exploited through a particular strategy, in which the arts and humanities—the very programs that face neglect nationally—would be stars of the show.

While USC has helped shape our digital age, its leadership and faculty have also been determined to inject a double dose of humanism, art, and culture into this technological era. In the process, experts in every field have gained immeasurably. Through the influx of exceptional students, faculty, and practitioners, the university's secret weapon in the arts was by 2015 well on its way to becoming a truly game-changing one.

Chapter 8

The Sun Never Sets on the Trojan Family

The Globalization of USC's Mission

For several years, USC's scholarly community had seen its future as connected to the powerful forces of globalization. Many leading American universities felt a similar need to build an academic profile befitting the era, but USC's case was special. It could aspire to be the country's first truly global university.

In one long and seminal age of human development, advances in culture occurred predominantly around the Mediterranean Sea. For centuries during the next pivotal age, such advances arose around the vast Atlantic Ocean. And as the 20th century gave way to a new one, observers noted another "shift in gravity"—this time to the vast and sprawling Pacific Rim and its diverse, growing societies. And just as certain institutions were able to hold outsized influence during the Mediterranean and Atlantic eras, USC was in a position to do so in the emerging Pacific Rim era.

USC's ability to assimilate international students has been a natural part of its character from the beginning. It had students from Japan in its first graduating class in 1884. And it has long been home to more international alumni and scholars than any other American university—many of them current (or potential future) leaders of the Pacific Rim. Given the presence of 350,000 USC alumni living around the world, President Nikias often quips, "You can say the sun never sets on the Trojan Family!"

Additionally, Los Angeles has emerged as a meaningful microcosm of America's new global context. Other U.S. cities may enjoy similar ethnic diversity, but none offers the same particular blend of Pacific-based cultures, which makes for a vibrant environment for learning, exploration, and experimentation. As Nikias has said, USC benefited simply by being at the emerging center of action in a post-Atlantic world; but it profited even more from being poised to capitalize on that setting, and thus to help bring shape and order to the larger processes of globalization.

While leading a USC delegation to Israel in 2012, President Nikias and First Lady Niki C. Nikias lay a wreath in the Hall of Remembrance at the Yad Vashem museum during a memorial ceremony honoring those lost in the Holocaust.

During USC's 2011 Global Conference in Hong Kong, President Nikias presents a gift and a USC letterman jacket to Pulitzer Prize–winning author Thomas Friedman, who served as the keynote speaker. They are flanked by then-Provost Elizabeth Garrett and Trustee Ronnie Chan.

Cinematic Arts dean Elizabeth Daley, former California governor Arnold Schwarzenegger, and filmmaker Joo-ick Lee take part in a panel on trends in global entertainment during USC's 2013 Global Conference in Seoul, South Korea. The former governor, who chairs the Schwarzenegger Institute for State and Global Policy at USC, delivered the conference's keynote address.

"The 224 languages that are spoken in this city, and the 115 nations represented today on this campus, are distinctly representative of a new world that is tilted toward the civilizations of the Pacific," Nikias said in his 2010 inaugural address. "This local microcosm of a new, global reality will help USC guide the tectonic shift that is already under way in this world."

Nikias also noted that if you drew a line from Chicago down through Texas on a map, USC and Stanford were the only two large, private research institutions west of that line. He argued that in a world leaning toward the Pacific Rim, USC now had a special opportunity, and even responsibility, to shape the intellectual and cultural fabric of the emerging global context.

In his inaugural address, before an audience of thousands of guests and university stakeholders, Nikias proposed in soaring terms the upper limits of what they could achieve as a global university:

> As our world today is shifting away from an Atlantic to a Pacific century, USC is better positioned than anyone else to lead this change: To become the intellectual and cultural and spiritual fabric of a world that is tied to the Age of the Pacific. To become the foremost laboratory of experimentation of "East-West" ideas, in scholarship and the arts and media and journalism and culture.

> To become the campus where the influencers of the Pacific age will be educated, shaped, and molded.

Nikias provocatively suggested that USC could hope to play a role analogous to the one Oxford University played in the Atlantic era, serving as an intellectual and cultural anchor for a world in flux.

Building Bridges Across Continents and Oceans

Toward the conclusion of Steven B. Sample's presidency in 2010, he and Nikias, then provost, led a delegation of USC officers and trustees across China to make academic inroads, establish research partnerships with leading

President Nikias gives Ratan Tata, head of the Tata Group, a personalized Trojan cricket jersey during an official USC delegation visit to India in 2011. Tata, a USC trustee, has been crucial to the university's efforts to collaborate with educational organizations across India. Seated on the right is Trustee Edward P. Roski Jr., who was then board chair.

Chinese institutions, and help recruit the best students of that nation. Soon after Nikias became president later that year, he committed USC to actively explore and execute new international partnerships and student recruitment efforts on a regular basis, in order to cement the university's status as a hub and anchor institution for our times.

Accordingly, USC's academic leadership moved quickly to visit Asia's other emerging giant, India, in the spring of 2011. President Nikias, then Board of Trustees chair Edward P. Roski Jr., and Trustee David Dornsife, along with other leaders, top faculty, and their spouses, traveled to Bangalore, India's high-tech capital; New Delhi, its political capital; and Mumbai, its financial capital, where they dedicated an international office. This latest outpost was in addition to previously established Asian outposts in Hong Kong and Shanghai. The USC Viterbi School of Engineering also soon opened a permanent office in Bangalore.

The delegation was hosted by Ratan Tata, a key international member of USC's Board of Trustees and the longtime head of India's venerable Tata Group. In New Delhi, Nikias and Tata had a private audience with Manmohan Singh, then prime minister, who years earlier had been the key architect of India's astonishing economic rise. During the meeting, Singh, mindful that USC alone was host to a remarkable 2,000 of the total 100,000 Indian students

Manmohan Singh (center), then prime minister of India, meets privately with Trustee Ratan Tata and President Nikias in New Delhi in 2011.

in America, told his Trojan guests, "Thank you for educating and looking after my people."

While the university was building ties with academic, business, and government leaders in India, the regional press gave it extensive attention. In the *Education Mail of New Delhi*, a major feature story made Indian citizens more familiar with USC's academic progress:

> [USC is] one of the world's leading private research universities, and is the most popular American university among Indian students....In the first-ever visit by a USC president to India, President C. L. Max Nikias came calling with a high-level delegation of USC deans. No less than Reliance Industries chair Mukesh Ambani threw a party for the delegation on their first day. The delegation was backed by USC trustee Ratan Tata, who also accompanied Nikias to meet Prime Minister Manmohan Singh.

The newspaper noted that Dean Varun Soni, who was part of the USC delegation, was an Indian-American with a Hindu and Buddhist background. "Soni created history in 2008 when he was appointed USC's dean of religious life," the *Mail* noted, "becoming the first Hindu and the first Indian ever to get such a post at a U.S. university. 'This is the first generation that lists meaning as one of the things they are looking for in their career, and our programming addresses this,' Soni said."

The India visit represented an intentional acceleration of USC's international activity. The number of global alliances and partnerships involving the university rose from about 148 in 2010 to 264 in 2015—a gain of more than 75 percent.

In 2012 a USC delegation led by Nikias and then-Provost Elizabeth Garrett visited Tel Aviv and Jerusalem, establishing academic partnerships

As the chair of the Association of Pacific Rim Universities in 2015, President Nikias presides over the organization's Annual Presidents Meeting in Osaka, Japan.

with a number of elite institutions, including the Technion-Israel Institute of Technology, Tel Aviv University, the Hebrew University of Jerusalem, and the Weizmann Institute of Science.

With USC trustee Alan Casden, President and Mrs. Nikias met with Shimon Peres, then Israel's president. And in a major event at the renowned Yad Vashem Holocaust History Museum, USC Shoah Foundation head Stephen D. Smith offered a presentation on the life-changing educational work that USC does through the foundation's Institute for Visual History and Education, and its treasure of 53,000 permanently archived, videotaped testimonies of Holocaust survivors.

Nikias views Latin America as an emerging region that rivals Asia in its future influence; he has noted that USC tripled the number of students from the area over the past several years and that more opportunity lies ahead. In 2013, he led a delegation of trustees and deans to Brazil, where they explored building academic partnerships, recruiting promising students, and raising support in Rio de Janeiro and São Paulo. USC officials also used the occasion to inaugurate an office in the latter city, which became the university's eighth permanent international post.

USC's leaders headed back to Asia in 2014, this time building ties in Singapore and Indonesia. Officials established partnerships with the National University of Singapore, one of the world's premier research institutions, as well as in medicine and business. They also traveled to the University of Indonesia and met with its leaders.

The USC president and first lady meet with Shimon Peres, then president of Israel, during a visit in 2012 by a delegation of university leaders to establish academic partnerships with leading institutions of that nation.

The delegation hosted a reception for Trojan parents and alumni in Singapore, as it often does on such trips, helping to connect them more deeply to the life of the university. The group also met with a number of local school headmasters to boost regional student recruitment. At the time of the trip, more than 80 students from Singapore and 161 from Indonesia were enrolled at USC, which reflected a 25 percent increase over the past five years. For the past half century, Indonesia has had a higher concentration of USC alumni among its society's leaders and influencers than nearly any other Asian nation.

Nikias also met with the leaders of the Association of Pacific Rim Universities, which is headquartered in Singapore. USC was a cofounding member of APRU, a Pacific Rim counterpart to the prestigious consortium of North American research universities known as the Association of American Universities. Later in 2014, at APRU's Annual Presidents Meeting in Canberra, Australia, Nikias was elected chair for a two-year term. In June 2015, he presided over one of the organization's most highly attended Presidents Meetings to date, in Osaka, Japan.

In the spring of 2015, USC officials flew to Mexico City, intent on making additional academic inroads there and, again, to pave the way for effective long-term recruiting of the region's best students. Among the highlights, USC and the Consejo Nacional de Ciencia y Tecnología (CONACYT)—Mexico's equivalent of the National Science Foundation—agreed to establish new funding for Mexican scholars, including 30 USC postdoctoral fellowships and five joint scholarships for students to pursue master's degrees at the Viterbi School of Engineering.

In Mexico City, Nikias honored José Antonio Meade Kuribreña, at that time the country's foreign secretary, with the inaugural Judge Widney Award. The accolade recognized Meade's leadership in establishing international

President and Mrs. Nikias meet with Mari Pangestu, the Indonesian minister of tourism and creative economy, during the 2014 delegation visit to Indonesia and Singapore. Pangestu, who is also a USC parent, spoke at an alumni reception in Jakarta.

educational diplomacy and building research partnerships between his country and the United States. Nikias also offered a keynote address at the Mexican Council of Foreign Relations on the subject of educational diplomacy.

Trojan Family Reunions—on a Global Scale

USC had, for years, hosted biannual Global Conferences in Asia, drawing together scholars, entrepreneurs, civic leaders, journalists, and policy makers to examine issues of mutual interest. The conferences increasingly drew hundreds of Trojan alumni and supporters from around the Pacific Rim, in addition to those from the United States who sought to build bridges to new opportunities in emerging economies.

The 2011 event, held in Hong Kong, became the most successful and well-attended USC Global Conference to date. Best-selling author and *New York Times* columnist Thomas Friedman keynoted the conference and met separately with USC leaders. The sold-out event drew 500 alumni from Indonesia, India, Sri Lanka, China, Japan, and across the region, allowing them to solidify a powerful international network.

In Nikias's inaugural address a year earlier, he had voiced an ambition to build special scholarship programs for students representing the various emerging Pacific societies and economies. "Let them take full advantage of a highly diverse environment they won't find anywhere else," he said, referring to USC's unique blend of the arts, humanities, and culture; science and technology; and the social sciences and professions. At the 2011 Global Conference, then-Provost Garrett was able to formally announce the International Artist Fellowship Program, which would bring some of the most promising talent to USC from around the world, particularly emphasizing Pacific Rim and Latin American nations.

During the 2015 Global Conference in Shanghai, President Nikias presents a Trojan letterman's jacket to keynote speaker Robert Iger, the CEO of Disney. Joining him onstage is Willow Bay, a veteran journalist and director of the USC School of Journalism.

Also coinciding with the conference, USC health and clinical leaders took a 10-day trip to explore healthcare delivery partnerships with top Chinese institutions. A number of USC schools went on to establish a major collaboration with partners at the renowned Shanghai Jiao Tong University the following year.

Seoul hosted the dynamic 2013 Global Conference, giving Trojans the ability to see up close the breathtaking rise of South Korea as an economic and cultural force. The keynote speaker was former California governor Arnold Schwarzenegger, who is a Governor Downey Professor and chair of the Schwarzenegger Institute for State and Global Policy at USC.

The 2015 Global Conference was held in Shanghai. It focused on innovations for a changing world, offering attendees a rare advance glimpse of where the greatest future opportunities would lie in business, science, health, technology, arts, and entertainment—and showcasing cutting-edge work by USC faculty in those areas. Disney CEO Robert Iger served as the conference's keynote speaker.

Furthering Global Conversation

In 2012, the year between USC's regular biennial Global Conferences, then-Provost Garrett hosted the university's first Global Conversation in London. Unlike the established conferences in Asia, Global Conversations were shorter

Students in the World Bachelor in Business program, a unique multi-continental program founded in 2013, give the “Fight On” sign. Participants in this highly competitive program spend an academic year in Los Angeles, Milan, and Hong Kong in order to gain insights into a rapidly globalizing economy.

events that gave Trojan Family members the ability to expand their networks in the capitals of the Atlantic region. Serving as the keynote speaker was the Right Honourable Jack Straw, a member of Parliament and the former home secretary, foreign secretary, and leader of the House of Commons under British prime minister Tony Blair.

New York City was the site for the 2014 Global Conversation, which helped showcase, to an East Coast audience, USC’s most advanced work in pivotal fields such as digital media, immersive and virtual reality, and bioengineering. Music and digital industry legend Jimmy Iovine, who had a year earlier co-established USC’s Jimmy Iovine and Andre Young Academy for Arts, Technology and the Business of Innovation, was the keynote speaker.

A Global—Yet Local—University

USC applied a particular method and discipline to its globalization efforts. While schools such as New York University were franchising their undergraduate programs in the Middle East, Asia, and other locations, USC was determined to avoid the satellite model, because its leadership believed that its Los Angeles campuses represented a mix of culture, energy, and opportunity that could not be replicated elsewhere.

However, while maintaining its core educational values, USC was still eager to experiment with inventive approaches to global education. In one major development, the USC Marshall School created a first-of-its-kind World Bachelor in Business (WBB) degree program. Its multi-continental curriculum connected elite business schools in three global cities—an alliance between USC, Hong Kong University of Science and Technology, and Bocconi University in Milan, Italy.

More than 400 applicants compete for the program's 40 spaces each year. In his regular column for *Bloomberg Business*, USC's renowned leadership expert Warren Bennis called the WBB program a true passport to the world. "Innovative is too bland a word," he wrote, "for what I consider an inspiring and unique breakthrough: the reframing of undergraduate business education with far-reaching and profound consequences."

The WBB partnership was just one way in which USC offered a unique, top-flight overseas study experience for students eager to gain a global perspective. In 2014, the university also partnered with a consortium of schools, including Cornell, Princeton, and the University of Hong Kong, to build a highly competitive program that sends undergraduates to study and work in a variety of dynamic East Asian cities.

Ultimately, USC's academic leadership charged every one of its schools to seek out international partnerships in education and scholarship, with a particular emphasis on emerging economies that could add considerable value to the Trojan student experience.

USC International Academy

As a way to augment its international recruitment, in 2013 the university established the USC International Academy. The program was designed by Vice President Anthony Bailey and others to ensure that the world's brightest non-English-speaking students were able to benefit from a USC education. It represented a merger and significant expansion of existing units, including the USC American Language Institute and USC Language Academy.

The initiative offered talented students conditional admission to various master's programs at USC, which they could enter upon successful completion of the International Academy. In its first year, it drew 1,100 students, more than double the number previously enrolled in its predecessor components.

In Mexico City in 2015, President Nikias and María Dolores Sánchez Soler of Consejo Nacional de Ciencia y Tecnología (CONACYT)—that nation's equivalent of the National Science Foundation—formalize an agreement to establish postdoctoral fellowships for Mexican scholars to study at USC.

Global University Governance

A global university needs leadership of a global scope. Years earlier, USC had become one of the first major American universities to elect foreign nationals to its governing board. This illustrious group included Ratan Tata, head of India's vast Tata Group; Ronnie Chan, chair of Hang Lung Group Limited and its subsidiary, Hang Lung Properties; Toshiaki Ogasawara, chair and publisher of *The Japan Times,* Japan's oldest English-language newspaper; and Y. H. Cho, chair and CEO of Korean Air and a founding member of SkyTeam, one of the world's fastest-growing airline alliances.

Since 2011, USC has added a number of key trustees from the world capitals where it aspires to be a growing academic force.

Chengyu Fu, a longtime leader of the Beijing-based China National Offshore Oil Corp. and former chair of Asia's largest refiner, Sinopec Group, was elected to the Board of Trustees in the fall of 2011, giving USC crucial representation within the corridors of what was becoming the world's largest economy. Fu, who holds a USC master's degree in petroleum engineering, was listed by *Harvard Business Review* as one of the 50 "Best-Performing CEOs in the World" in 2010.

The next year, Daniel M. Tsai, chair of Fubon Financial, Taiwan's second largest financial services group, joined the Board of Trustees. Over the last half century, Fubon Financial has evolved from a property-and-casualty-insurance provider into a giant of the banking, securities, life insurance, and asset-management business.

The board welcomed Dominic Ng, chair and CEO of East West Bank, to its ranks in 2014. Born and raised in Hong Kong, Ng had served on the university's President's Leadership Council since 2013 and has been a tireless supporter of the USC Pacific Asia Museum. He has been named one of

President Nikias signs a memorandum of understanding with Edson Aparecido, chief secretary of the government of São Paulo, during a USC delegation visit to Brazil in 2013.

"25 Notable Chinese-Americans" by *Forbes*, one of the "100 Most Influential People in L.A." by the *Los Angeles Times*, and "Business Person of the Year" by the *Los Angeles Business Journal.*

At this moment in history, the need for genuinely global research universities is greater than ever before, due to rapid societal and technological changes. In a globalized age, such institutions can guide debates about public policy, generate economic value, and explore old problems from new vantage points. But equally crucial is the need for any student graduating in the coming years to be prepared for a world in which both competition and opportunity lie in far-flung places that had been less relevant to the goals and successes of previous generations. By 2015, USC had gone a considerable way toward becoming a model for such a university. But its progress only hinted at the deeper cross-continental educational connections that could and would be created with sustained effort.

Luminaries and nearly 1,000 attendees gathered on campus for the opening symposium of the USC Schwarzenegger Institute for State and Global Policy in September 2012. The event featured examinations of potential post-partisan solutions to pressing policy issues. From left: ABC political commentator Cokie Roberts, Senator John McCain, and former Senate majority leader Tom Daschle.

Chapter 9

A Convening Place for the World

Serving as a Vibrant Crossroads

Near the base of the steps to USC's stately Doheny Memorial Library is a plaque placed by the student body, commemorating a convocation address given there by John Fitzgerald Kennedy on November 1, 1960. One week later, Kennedy became the youngest person elected to the United States presidency.

That season, in fact, saw two future presidents at the university, as Richard M. Nixon had appeared on campus a few weeks before. USC also hosted William Taft, Franklin Delano Roosevelt, and Gerald Ford when each was in office.

Over the following years, USC brought figures of national and international standing to its campuses with increasing frequency; it also represented the Trojan presence in the places where leaders were shaping the world, from state and national capitals to cultural and financial centers across the globe.

"We take our role seriously as a university that is a crossroads and convening place for the world's most important discussions," said Tom Sayles, senior vice president for university relations. "There's no reason we shouldn't play that role in a stronger way than ever, especially given our location in Southern California, one of the major capitals of this new Pacific century. So we bring important people to campus—and many times, we go out to where they are, to discuss with them how we can work with them to face some of society's biggest challenges."

Bringing the World to USC

Following through on this mission, in recent years USC has hosted a number of sitting and former presidents, along with a range of other public servants, spiritual leaders, decorated military officers, and VIPs.

President Barack Obama came to campus in 2010 at the invitation of the students, drawing more than 35,000 members of the academic and local

TOP LEFT: President Nikias, former president George W. Bush, and USC board chair John Mork meet during the Bushes' 2013 visit to campus. USC Marshall School dean James G. Ellis interviewed the Bushes as part of the USC President's Distinguished Lecture series.

BOTTOM LEFT: After giving formal remarks, former president Bill Clinton discusses foreign affairs challenges and other topics with Dean Ellis in another USC President's Distinguished Lecture series event in November 2014.

communities to a massive outdoor event in front of Doheny Memorial Library.

The 42nd and 43rd American presidents made featured appearances as part of USC's President's Distinguished Lecture series. In November 2013, the university hosted George and Laura Bush at a full Bovard Auditorium. Bush offered reflections on momentous events during his years in office as well as insights into his life after leaving the White House, while the former first lady discussed her work in promoting literacy, expanding educational access to women, and advancing human rights.

The following November, USC welcomed Bill Clinton, who shared his analysis of a new "interdependent" global context, which he said required a shift in the manner in which the United States exercised leadership. Former senator and secretary of state Hillary Rodham Clinton was a special guest on campus in March 2013.

Shinzo Abe, prime minister of Japan, made a high-profile visit to the campus, where he had been a student in the 1970s, in May 2015. A little more

Laura Bush and Niki C. Nikias share personal memories during a visit from the former U.S. president and first lady to the university in the fall of 2013.

than a month later, he returned the favor and received President Nikias as a guest in Tokyo. Later that year Ghana's president, John Dramani Mahama, spoke on campus at the invitation of USC's Center on Public Diplomacy.

While many VIP visits were brief, some led to lasting bonds that created academic opportunities for Trojans. In the summer of 2012, former California governor Arnold Schwarzenegger established the USC Schwarzenegger Institute for State and Global Policy, dedicated to fostering a post-partisan approach to policy issues. He took on the title of the Governor Downey Professor of State and Global Policy while also serving as the chair of the institute's board of advisers. He also delivered the keynote at USC's 2013 Global Conference in Seoul.

In May 2015, former British prime minister Gordon Brown appeared as a guest lecturer in Professor Steve Lamy's undergraduate seminar "Case Studies in Modern Leadership," analyzing economic and cultural issues of global scope—while also taking the time to chat personally with almost every student in attendance.

Retired four-star general and former CIA director David Petraeus became a member of the Trojan academic community in 2013, taking on the role of a Judge Widney Professor, with a joint appointment at the USC Price

President John Dramani Mahama of Ghana meets with President Nikias in October 2015. The African nation's head of state was a guest of the USC Center on Public Diplomacy, which had invited him to discuss his country and its export efforts.

Filmmaker and USC trustee Steven Spielberg greets Holocaust survivor Mira Becker at an event announcing a new genocide research center at the USC Shoah Foundation Institute. Nikias, while provost, was instrumental in bringing the institute, which was founded by Spielberg in 1994, to the university in 2006.

School of Public Policy. During one weeklong visit in 2014, he mentored Price School undergraduate and graduate students, led ROTC cadets on a morning run in the historic Los Angeles Memorial Coliseum, paid visits to the Keck School of Medicine's trauma training unit, and lectured at the USC Marshall School of Business.

The university also began to make use of its affiliated Sunnylands estate in Rancho Mirage, California, to host events of global import. Envisioned by the late Walter and Leonore Annenberg as a "West Coast Camp David," the 200-acre property serves as an ideal retreat site for world leaders to explore key issues at length. In 2013, Sunnylands hosted the famous "shirt-sleeves summit," where President Barack Obama and Chinese president Xi Jinping were able to improve bonds as the United States turned its attention increasingly from the Atlantic to the Pacific.

Not all the VIPs who appeared at USC came from the traditional halls of political power. In 2011, the 14th Dalai Lama delighted students, staff, and faculty with wisdom and spiritual insights. His appearance at multiple campus events was a part of his first visit to the United States after giving up his political duties for Tibet's government in exile.

Bringing USC to the World

USC doesn't just bring big shows to campus: It often takes the show on the road, through official delegations and USC Global Conferences, to places that are growing in academic importance to the university.

In recent years, senior delegations to India, Israel, Brazil, Indonesia, Singapore, and Mexico met with high-ranking public officials, civic leaders, and policy makers. In New Delhi in 2011, President Nikias and Trustee Ratan Tata had a private audience with Manmohan Singh, then India's prime minister. In Israel in 2012, the Nikiases met with then-President Shimon Peres. And in 2015, Nikias honored José Antonio Meade Kuribreña, then Mexico's foreign secretary, with the inaugural Judge Widney Award.

Water in the West

RIGHT: USC celebrates a $10 million gift to its School of Cinematic Arts from Sumner Redstone (center), the former executive chair of Viacom Inc. and CBS Corp. With him are (from left) Cinematic Arts dean Elizabeth Daley, Trustee Steven Spielberg, Trustee Frank Price, alumnus George Lucas, and President Nikias.

Domestically, USC's leadership meets regularly with key policy makers at the local, state, and national levels. Each year these delegations, including senior administrators, trustees, and key faculty, visit both Sacramento and Washington, D.C. During the 2012 trip to California's capital, President Nikias held an hour-long meeting with Governor Jerry Brown to discuss developments at the university. In 2015, Nikias led another state capital visit to educate policy makers on how extending Cal Grant support to low- and middle-income students at private universities serves Californians.

In 2012, USC's delegation to Washington met with a host of high-ranking officials to discuss healthcare, innovation, civic engagement, and other issues of mutual interest. The university representatives spent time with government leaders including then-Senate Majority Leader Harry Reid; House Minority Leader Nancy Pelosi; Hawaiian senator Daniel Inouye; and Martha Kanter, who was then undersecretary of the U.S. Department of Education.

In the spring of 2015, Nikias and Provost Michael Quick led another group of trustees, senior administrators, and deans to the nation's capital. The USC officials promoted the work of the university's faculty in vital areas such as health and medicine, cybersecurity, digital media, and national and homeland security.

A Campus Where Stars Constellate

When USC launched the Visions & Voices initiative in 2006, the intention was to direct the spotlight onto its world-class arts and humanities programs. The ultimate goal, as Nikias, who was at that time provost, put it, was "not merely to entertain our students but to bring out the full educational value of the arts, and to challenge them at the core of their being about what it means for us to live together as human beings in society."

TOP LEFT: Japanese prime minister Shinzo Abe, who studied at USC, enjoys a walk through the campus in May 2015, accompanied by President Nikias, Japan's first lady, Akie Abe, and the university's first lady, Niki C. Nikias.

MIDDLE LEFT: U.S. Supreme Court Justice Antonin Scalia, with President Nikias during a 2012 visit to USC, when he also lectured and met with law students; Supreme Court Justice Anthony Kennedy is welcomed to campus by Robert Rasmussen (then dean of the Gould School of Law) and Nikias in 2011.

BOTTOM LEFT: Los Angeles mayor Eric Garcetti, Provost Michael Quick, President Nikias, and Sol Price School of Public Policy dean Jack Knott meet with General Martin Dempsey, chair of the Joint Chiefs of Staff; California governor Jerry Brown and Nikias meet to discuss the state's approach to water conservation.

TOP: Former secretary of defense Robert Gates, now chancellor of the College of William & Mary, arrives on campus to offer a 2012 installment of the USC President's Distinguished Lecture series.

BOTTOM: The Nikiases welcome former British prime minister Gordon Brown in the spring of 2015. Brown spent two weeks on campus as a guest of international relations professor Steven Lamy to participate in his course "Case Studies in Modern Leadership."

Former Los Angeles mayor Antonio Villaraigosa (center), who joined the USC faculty as a professor of the practice of policy within the Price School of Public Policy in 2013, meets with LAPD chief Charlie Beck (left) and President Nikias at City Hall in 2012.

Over the years, Visions & Voices has drawn many luminaries to campus through a variety of programs, especially its Signature Events series. Highlights have included musician and writer Patti Smith, who discussed her wide-ranging career in a conversation moderated by USC Annenberg School professor Joshua Kun in February 2013. In the fall of that year, students competed lottery-style for 1,235 seats in Bovard Auditorium, where Sir Elton John performed with 40 student musicians from the USC Thornton School of Music in a concert dubbed "Elton John Goes Back to School."

Beyond Visions & Voices, of course, a variety of USC programs have pulled many other stars into the university's orbit, both for collaborative

LEFT: President and Mrs. Nikias greet Texas governor Greg Abbott—the parent of a USC undergraduate—during a visit by the governor to the University Park Campus.

performances and in recognition of public service. For example, in April 2015, Fleetwood Mac guitarist and songwriter Lindsey Buckingham was a guest of the Lloyd Greif Center for Entrepreneurial Studies. During his visit, he spoke to students and performed with the Trojan Marching Band in Bovard Auditorium.

The USC School of Social Work honored actor Gary Sinise with its Crystal Heart in 2011 for his support of American troops. The relationship continued when in March 2014, the social work school and the Gary Sinise Foundation co-hosted a conference examining the challenges facing wounded veterans and caregivers.

Each year, the USC Shoah Foundation presents its Ambassador for Humanity Award. At the 2013 annual gala, the organization honored actor George Clooney; the following year, Trustee Steven Spielberg presented the award to President Barack Obama. When William Clay Ford Jr., executive chair of Ford Motor Company, received the award in 2015, actor Steve Carell emceed the gala, which also featured appearances by Oscar-winning actress Halle Berry and singer James Taylor.

The innumerable and ongoing interactions with so many of the world's most influential citizens energized the USC community and infused it with a sense of limitless possibility. And the university's continuous growth—in terms of academics, reputation, cultural diversity, and even physical infrastructure—ensured that it would remain a bustling crossroads for years to come.

TOP RIGHT: Actor and humanitarian George Clooney (center) receives the Ambassador for Humanity Award from the USC Shoah Foundation in 2013, flanked by President and Mrs. Nikias, Trustee Steven Spielberg, and Shoah Foundation director Stephen D. Smith; Sir Elton John performs with USC student musicians at a 2013 Visions & Voices Signature Event.

MIDDLE RIGHT: Award-winning entertainer Rita Moreno speaks at a 2014 Visions & Voices event celebrating her storied career; President Nikias and international soccer star and UNICEF ambassador David Beckham are honored at the annual UNICEF Ball in 2016, with UNICEF chair Ghada Irani and Caryl Stern, president and CEO of the U.S. Fund for UNICEF.

BOTTOM RIGHT: USC Social Work dean Marilyn Flynn and President Nikias present actor Gary Sinise with the Crystal Heart, the school's highest honor for community service; award-winning director Spike Lee appears at a Visions & Voices event.

TNT

children first.

SC

Honorary Degree Recipients 2010–2015

Since 1912, USC has used its spring commencement exercise as an occasion to bestow honorary degrees on women and men who have made extraordinary contributions to scholarship, society, culture, and the life and mission of the university. In the past five years, this has included major global figures drawn from the worlds of the arts, sciences, philanthropy, media, athletics, and industry.

** Asterisks denote commencement speakers*

2015: Famed NFL and former USC football coach Pete Carroll with Athletic Director Pat Haden and Provost Michael Quick

2012: Christiane Amanpour,* award-winning news correspondent

2014: Shonda L. Rhimes, television producer and USC alumna, with then-Provost Elizabeth Garrett and President Nikias

2010: Steven Ballmer,* former CEO of Microsoft

2014: B. Wayne Hughes Sr., USC trustee and alumnus, and renowned business leader

2014: Marc Benioff,* USC trustee and alumnus, and CEO of Salesforce

2015: Ariel Investments president Mellody Hobson,* USC alumnus and benefactor George Lucas, and California attorney general Kamala Harris, with President and Mrs. Nikias

2013: Jimmy Iovine,* music producer and philanthropist, with then-Provost Elizabeth Garrett and President Nikias

2011: Harald zur Hausen, Nobel Prize-winning virologist, with Keck School of Medicine dean Carmen Puliafito

2011: Girish Karnad, acclaimed actor, director, and playwright

2013: Award-winning playwright David Henry Hwang with President Nikias

"All the News
...Fit to Print"

U.S.C. President

By BILLY WITZ

LOS ANGELES — The University of Southern California swiftly rebuked the key figures who helped land its athletic program on probation, firing the athletic director Mike Garrett, returning Reggie Bush's Heisman Trophy, and beefing up the compliance staff. The university also plans to remove from campus jerseys and murals of Bush and the basketball star O. J. Mayo.

The university's president-elect, Max Nikias, announced the moves Tuesday in a letter he sent to university boosters. They are effective Aug. 3, when Nikias replaces Dr. Steven Sample, who is retiring.

"U.S.C., which experiences both the opportunities and challenges involved with a high-profile athletics program at a global hub, will seek to excel in the coming years in a manner that is consistent with the highest values of the academy," Nikias wrote.

As if to underscore that point, Nikias replaced Garrett with Pat Haden, an NBC broadcaster who is a Rhodes scholar and former star quarterback for the Trojans. Haden resigned his post as a member of U.S.C.'s board of trustees to accept the job.

Haden said he wanted to hire J. K. McKay, his former receiver and the son of the former U.S.C. coach John McKay, as a liaison between himself and the

Chapter 10

The Renewal of the Trojan Empire

Athletics Builds on Its Glorious Heritage

USC's legendary athletics program is the "glue that holds the worldwide Trojan Family together," President Nikias said in his October 2010 inaugural address. And he pledged that in the coming years, "We will celebrate a Trojan heritage of student athletics that will be more glorious than before. Yes, our Trojan student-athletes are indeed students first and foremost. And so our athletic heritage will demonstrate that the triumphs of athletics and the triumphs of education are the same, at their core. Body and mind, working together, in pursuit of excellence."

However, college sports, one decade into the 21st century, was a national enterprise in rapid flux. Many journalists, faculty, and others around the country questioned the role of "big-time sports" on campus, as successful college teams could now be as complex and high-stakes as professional ones.

A few months before Nikias's address, in the summer of 2010, USC had found itself at the center of the storm. The National Collegiate Athletic Association (NCAA) handed down penalties on the Trojan football program for violations that had been committed five years earlier. The sanctions were largely in response to allegations that former USC football star Reggie Bush had received improper benefits from sports agents who hoped to cash in on his expected future professional success. Additional charges against the overall athletics program involved basketball player O. J. Mayo, who was also ruled to have taken benefits from outsiders during his one season at USC.

The NCAA's Committee on Infractions charged the university with insufficient oversight and penalized it heavily, in ways that critics would increasingly call excessive over the coming years. These sanctions called for USC to vacate a number of past wins; to sit out two seasons of bowl eligibility; to lose 30 football scholarships over three seasons; and to disassociate from Bush and Mayo.

President-elect Nikias faced a delicate but vital balancing act: He sought

In July 2010, media across the nation reported dramatic changes in USC's athletics department, as a new president prepared to lead the Trojan athletic program into a stage of revitalization.

In a widely praised move in his first days in office, President Nikias brought back USC football legends Pat Haden (left) and J. K. McKay (right) to oversee a new era in Trojan athletics.

The Trojan Warrior presides over the Hall of Champions, the centerpiece of USC's renovated Heritage Hall, which underwent a multimillion-dollar program of enhancements in 2013 before reopening the following year.

to ensure that USC's athletic tradition would remain committed to the highest levels of excellence and achievement, while also addressing perceptions that the Trojans could have been more diligent in overseeing compliance with NCAA rules.

Nikias would later recount that—though many observers saw the severity of the sanctions as unprecedented and unfair—he had needed to move swiftly to protect the integrity and reputation of a university that had come so far in recent years.

On the morning of July 21, 2010, about two weeks before he officially assumed office, Nikias released an announcement detailing a number of actions he would take as president. Chief among them was bringing in Pat Haden as the new athletic director. A university trustee, Trojan football icon, Rhodes scholar, and respected businessman and broadcaster, Haden immediately brought a fresh tone to Heritage Hall, the home of USC Athletics. Nikias also announced the formation of a larger and stronger compliance team, headed by esteemed lawyer David Roberts. Both Roberts and Haden would begin their posts on August 3—the same day as President Nikias.

Nikias also stated that USC would return Bush's 2005 Heisman Trophy. It was one of seven Heismans displayed in Heritage Hall—a number that

had temporarily tied the university with Notre Dame and Ohio State for the most won by its players. As Nikias explained, "The Trojan Family honors and respects [only] the USC sporting careers of those persons whose actions did not compromise their athletic program or the opportunities of future USC student-athletes."

The actions drew notice in the national media and sports community as a sign that USC would be aggressive and unflinching in how it moved forward. "Credit to the new guy, president-elect Max Nikias," wrote *Los Angeles Times* columnist and former sports editor Bill Dwyre. "He either knew or listened to

the right people. Either way, he got it right. . . . Haden is a once-in-a-lifetime person who transcends fan loyalty and school bias. He's a class act."

"USC President-Elect Cleans House," read *The New York Times* headline on a major story about the announcements. "USC, which experiences both the opportunities and challenges involved with a high-profile athletics program at a global hub, will seek to excel in the coming years in a manner that is consistent with the highest values of the academy," it quoted the incoming president as saying. And ESPN wrote, "Though he doesn't start his new job until August 3, Nikias is already at work reforming the Trojans' image."

In the face of unprecedented adversity over an extended period of NCAA sanctions and penalties, the USC football team played with uncommon pride and passion, poising itself for a swift return to national prominence.

President Nikias frequently meets with USC's student-athletes to teach and encourage them on and off the field. Here he draws upon his Greek heritage to remind football players of the deeper meaning of the ancient legends of the Trojans.

New Era, New Leadership

Seeing the athletics program through the period of NCAA-mandated sanctions and probation was one of the most crucial jobs of the new administration. Even in a small college town, it's hard to keep tabs on whether student-athletes may be hearing the siren songs of unscrupulous sports agents or overeager boosters. Under the bright lights of Los Angeles, and with an active media, the task is far more difficult. And this time, an infraction of NCAA amateurism rules could have resulted in catastrophic, long-term penalties. But, led by Haden, and Roberts and his compliance office, USC came through probation safely; in fact, Trojan athletics on the whole had been renewed and strengthened. The facilities, coaches, and support were now in place for enduring success.

In recognition of Nikias's efforts to renew USC's athletics heritage, in 2010 *The New York Times* named him one of a small number of national figures "who make sports' little corner of the world a better place."

"After Major Probation, USC's Compliance Office Among Best in Nation," read a June 2014 headline in the *Los Angeles Times*. "At the time USC was penalized [in the summer of 2010]," the article noted, "the university had five compliance employees. Now, it is twice that size—among the largest in

AAA.com
State Farm

Trojans
SC

USC's storied football program has maintained its strength and prestige through several years of transition.

TOP LEFT: President Nikias and Athletic Director Pat Haden visit with Lane Kiffin (center), head coach from 2010 to 2013. Kiffin's organizational skill and planning allowed the Trojans to navigate sanctions while maintaining winning records and high expectations. His tenure included a 10–2 record in 2011, punctuated by a 50–0 drubbing of rival UCLA.

TOP RIGHT: Ed Orgeron led the Trojans to a 6–2 record as interim head coach in 2013, which included a dramatic last-second win over fifth-ranked Stanford.

BOTTOM: Clay Helton served two successful stints as USC's interim head coach. He led the Trojans to a 45–20 victory over Fresno State in the Las Vegas Bowl at the conclusion of the 2013 season. After again assuming the interim head coach role midway through the 2015 season, he guided the team to a 5–2 record, a significant victory over UCLA, and the championship of the Pac-12 conference's southern division. After the UCLA game, Athletic Director Pat Haden named him USC's permanent head coach.

college sports. Administrators also have worked to foster a relationship with NCAA leadership and to be transparent when things do inevitably go wrong."

Fighting on, Against the Odds

The NCAA's sanctions were unusually severe in proportion to the allegations, which led both fans and the media to repeatedly raise issues of fairness and consistency in the following years. Yet USC's approach was to emulate the attitude of the ancient Trojan warriors, even under the most severe pressure. As Nikias advised members of the football team at training camp during one season of the sanction period, "Fight on, and do not complain to the media or the public about the unfairness. Just fight like champions."

Nikias, the Greco-Roman classicist, often reminded the student-athletes that the very spirit of being a Trojan involved a relish for challenges that others avoid, a thirst to conquer obstacles from which others retreat. At the outset of his presidency, word among the university's rivals and competitors was that USC athletics had been "dealt a fatal blow," he said. But he exhorted student-athletes to take inspiration from the determination of the ancient Trojans, to "fight on against all odds, and even bend the will of the gods in their favor."

And—against the odds—the next years were some of the most productive for Trojan sports. One key victory came in fundraising: Between 2010 and 2015, despite the soft economy, supporters contributed $300 million in financial donations for student-athletes, Trojan teams, and training facilities—an all-time school record.

This income funded some much-needed improvements. While USC's student-athlete program capitalized on its location in the dynamic city of Los Angeles, many schools in less-glamorous settings could boast facilities that were far more modern and expansive.

In 2011, the university began construction on a $70 million sports complex that was designed not simply to make up ground that had been lost to rivals but to move past them. The new John McKay Center opened its doors just a year later, attracting substantial media attention. "It sends a message nationally," Nikias said. "It makes a statement about how USC intends to be the single greatest destination for those who aspire to make their mark athletically and academically and in life."

Following NCAA sanctions in 2010, David Roberts joined USC as vice president of athletic compliance. Within a few years, the university's compliance programs were cited as among the best in the nation.

As a student-athlete, Cynthia Cooper-Dyke helped lead the USC women's basketball team to two national titles. Returning as its coach in 2013, she led the team to its first-ever Pac-12 championship, and its first NCAA tournament berth in nearly a decade.

In addition to guiding the McKay Center to rapid completion, Athletics Director Haden led the renovation of USC's venerable program headquarters, Heritage Hall, as well as the upgrading of the Uytengsu Aquatics Center, among other capital projects.

Haden also pressed the notion that USC's sports participants should be fully engaged in the social and cultural life of the university and promoted community service in particular. By 2015, annual volunteer work by student-athletes exceeded 4,000 hours collectively, a new school record, through more than 300 separate events serving the local community.

Athletic Achievements and New Frontiers

In the first five years that Haden served as athletic director, the Trojans won 10 national championships in team sports and 32 in individual competition. During this time, the school also was home to five Academic All-American first-teamers; four Honda Sports Award winners (honoring the best female student-athletes in a dozen different sports); and three Crosstown Cup trophies, which recognize the annual winner of overall athletic competition between USC and its neighboring rival UCLA.

In London in 2012, USC—already the top producer of Olympic competitors and medalists among American universities—celebrated its most

successful Games ever. Trojan athletes competed in seven sports, representing 18 nations. They won 25 medals, a new USC record, and the highest number for competitors from any school. Among these were 12 golds, meaning that the university's gold-medal-winning streak, dating back to 1912, now spanned a full century. Had it stood as its own nation, the school would have placed sixth in the gold-medal standings and 11th overall.

USC had publicly committed to future successes in athletics that would be as bright or even brighter than ever. This effort involved an unceasing quest for excellence in those sports that the university had historically dominated, but it also meant getting into the game in new activities that were growing in

popularity. Among these was lacrosse, which enjoyed a high profile at many of the Ivy League schools with which USC was increasingly competing in the academic arena. Accordingly, Nikias established funding for a women's Division I lacrosse team, with plans for a men's team later.

Haden, meanwhile, introduced women's sand volleyball to the athletic program in 2012, and a court was created on the eastern edge of the University Park Campus. The new team quickly came to dominate the sport, winning the AVCA national title in 2015.

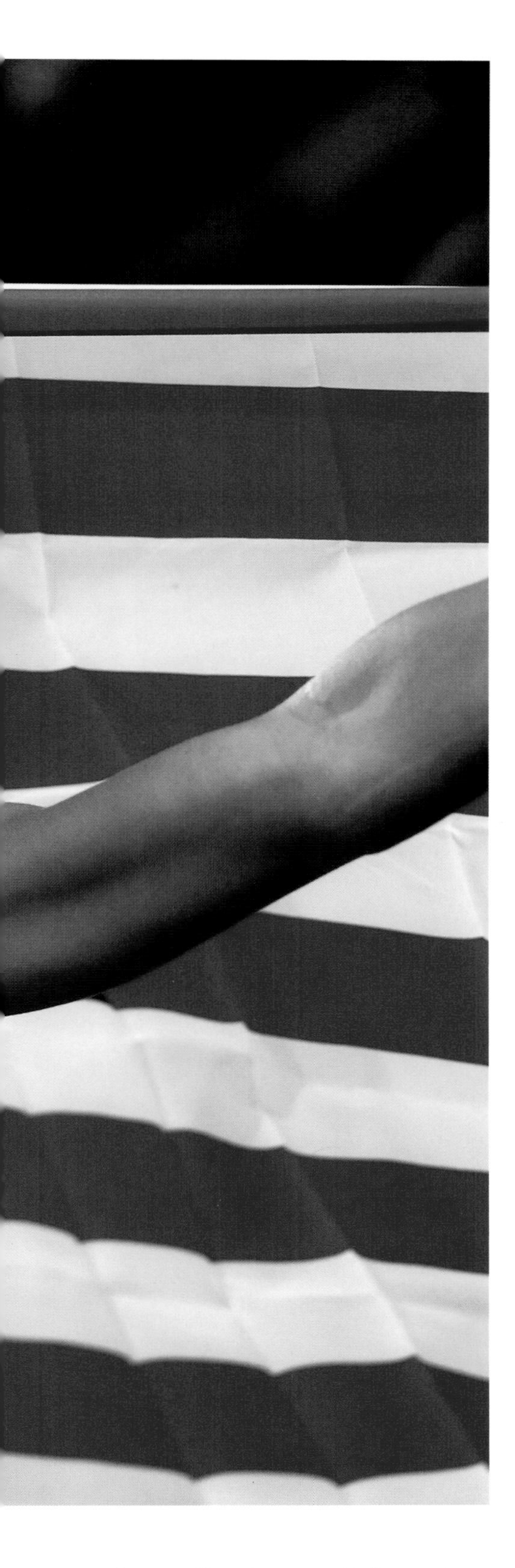

Trojan swimmer Rebecca Soni celebrates one of her two gold-medal victories in London. Soni has won a total of six Olympic medals (including three gold), six NCAA titles, and a roomful of other medals and trophies.

At the 2012 Olympic Games, Trojan track star Allyson Felix wins a gold medal in the 200-meter dash for the United States. USC athletes added to the university's unparalleled Olympic record by bringing home 25 medals from London—more than any other school that year, and the most ever for USC.

Two of USC's marquee programs underwent overhauls in April 2013, when Haden hired Andy Enfield and Cynthia Cooper-Dyke as head coaches of the Trojan men's and women's basketball teams, respectively.

Cooper was already a Trojan icon, who as a student-athlete helped lead USC to two national titles. She was also an Olympic gold medalist, the winner of four WNBA titles, a member of both the USC Athletics Hall of Fame and the WNBA Hall of Fame—and now a coach who had lifted three separate programs to new levels of excellence. Making an immediate impact, she guided the Trojan team to some of its strongest seasons in years, including a Pac-12 title tournament and NCAA berth in 2014.

Enfield had made his name as the architect of the high-flying Florida Gulf Coast team that became the first 15-seed in history to make the Sweet Sixteen round of the NCAA tournament. At USC, he gradually rebuilt the Trojan program into an exciting athletic club that began to gain national attention as the 2015–2016 season unfolded.

Triumphantly Weathering the Storm

In the years following the 2010 sanctions against the Trojan football program, journalists and sports observers increasingly noted that in proportion to the

USC men's basketball began a major rebuilding effort in 2013 when it brought in Andy Enfield, a rising star in the coaching ranks of college basketball, to serve as head coach.

Jovan Vavic, coach of both the women's and men's water polo teams at USC, celebrates one of six consecutive national titles with his men's team.

violations that the NCAA had found, USC had been penalized more severely than any school in history.

In 2011, ESPN's Ted Miller wrote, tellingly, of an encounter at an airport with an administrator from a rival athletics program: "He told me, after some small talk and off-the-record, that 'everybody' thought USC got screwed." The administrator had voiced that "USC was punished for its 'USC-ness,'" which included a resentment of the way the media glamorized the university, its Los Angeles environs, and its popularity with celebrities.

Two years later, Miller wrote about his own continuing frustrations about the inconsistency of the NCAA's dealings with USC. He recounted that at one point, while talking to Haden, "I started to rant about USC's NCAA case. You know what Haden said? 'Let it go,' he told me. And he was right."

During the probationary years, the president and first lady took the Trojan football team under their wings. The Nikiases were a constant presence on the sidelines, whether at the Coliseum, or in South Bend, Indiana, or East Rutherford, New Jersey. They missed only one game, which coincided with USC's biennial Global Conference in Asia. During the two years that the university wasn't eligible to participate in a bowl game, they hosted the team at President's House in San Marino for a December holiday party, to express

their appreciation for how the student-athletes represented USC during these difficult times.

The football team fought on admirably through the probation, though during four of those five seasons, it often had 15 to 20 fewer players available than opposing teams—due to scholarship cuts and an NCAA injunction that allowed USC players to transfer to other schools with the promise of immediate eligibility.

The team, led by new coach Lane Kiffin, in 2010 posted 8 wins, and in 2011, a highly successful 10-win, top-10-ranked season, which led to overly

USC launched two new women's athletic teams in recent years, both quickly achieving success. The women's sand volleyball program was introduced in 2012 and, just three years later, won its first national championship. In 2013, the university launched women's lacrosse.

high expectations within the media for the following year. The 2012 team finished with a 7–6 tally. The 2013 team managed an almost miraculous 10–4 record, during a time marked by instability and coaching changes. The ability of the Trojans to embrace uncertainty manifested decisively on the field that fall. During the final year of sanctions, 2014, Steve Sarkisian took the helm as head coach and led the team to a 9-win finish.

Many observers viewed the five years affected by scholarship cuts as a "virtual death penalty." Yet USC had not even one losing season. Every other major program that had faced such a degree of sanctions had posted at least one losing record during their penalties. The Trojans had indeed fought on.

USC finished those five searingly difficult seasons with a total of 44 wins and 21 losses. That compared favorably with performances over the same years by archrivals Notre Dame (45–20) and UCLA (39–27)—even though each of those programs was undergoing a renaissance—as well as another traditional powerhouse, the University of Texas Longhorns (36–28).

When USC met Notre Dame in the Coliseum in November 2014, it marked the last regular season game in which the football team would labor under the sanctions. The Trojans won convincingly, 49–14. They next took on the storied Nebraska Cornhuskers in the 2014 Holiday Bowl in San Diego. USC prevailed 45–42, and then set its sights on the future.

Clockwise from top left: The USC men's basketball team has been reinvigorated under new coach Andy Enfield; women's soccer has twice reached the NCAA tournament in recent years; Trojan track and field squads are stocked with current NCAA champions and future Olympic heroes; Tommy Trojan and mascot Traveler; hurdler Felix Sanchez, also known as "The Invincible" and "Superman," takes the gold in the 2012 Olympics.

Clockwise from top left: Bryshon Nellum earned a silver medal in London—just a few years after doctors told him that a leg injury would keep him from returning to elite status—and was chosen to carry the American flag at the closing ceremony; Trojan swimmers and divers have won 19 titles over the last five seasons; USC tennis has captured four team championships and three singles and doubles titles since 2010; a USC pitcher plies his trade at Dedeaux Field; the USC women's crew team prepares for action.

Todd Dickey, senior vice president of administration, guided negotiations that led to USC taking on a 98-year master lease for the Los Angeles Memorial Coliseum in 2013. Two years later, USC announced plans to restore and renovate the venerable stadium.

Within a few months, that future looked considerably brighter. No sooner had the NCAA penalties been lifted than the Trojan football program found itself in a position that had been quite familiar for it during most of the previous 15 years: USC signed the top group of high-school recruits in the nation, by several analysts' measure, dramatically demonstrating the enduring power of the university's brand in athletics.

The 2015 season involved growing pains for the USC football program, though the ultimate result was a stable new coaching regime led by longtime assistant Clay Helton and a decisive victory over rival UCLA. After a narrow loss to a solid Wisconsin squad in the Holiday Bowl, the Trojans began preparations for a season-opening 2016 showdown against national champion Alabama, a match that would certainly be a benchmark for a program intent on returning to the apex of the college football world.

The Long View

As the landscape of intercollegiate sports continued to experience seismic pressure waves and shifts, President Nikias regularly urged the student-athletes to make the most of their USC experience, and to understand how it would fit into the larger scope of their lives. In meetings held at the beginning of each school year with all the incoming sports program participants, the president offered context for the role of athletics today at a great research university. The ancient model, he said, went back to the Greeks' original Olympic games, which celebrated both physical and intellectual achievements as the essence of civilization. In the first of these annual speeches, he said:

> The athletic quest was not divorced from the intellectual quest in that great ancient society, which gave birth to so much of modern civilization. They believed that for human beings to reach their potential, they had to achieve excellence in the mind and body

USC National Championships 2010–2015

In 127 years of intercollegiate athletic competition, USC teams have won 97 national titles in men's sports and 26 in women's sports, more than all but two other schools. Between 2010 and 2015 alone, the university's student-athletes won 11 NCAA championships in team sports. This success came at the same moment that USC was undergoing dramatic academic growth, confirming the Trojan community's belief that excellence in athletic competition breeds excellence in all other areas of a great university's mission.

Men's Water Polo: NCAA Champions, 2010, 2011, 2012, 2013

Women's Sand Volleyball: AVCA title, 2015

Men's Tennis: NCAA Champions, 2010, 2011, 2012, 2014

Women's Water Polo: NCAA Champions, 2010, 2013

Women's Golf: NCAA Champions, 2013

> and spirit. Excellence in all things: Like no other university community in America, the USC Trojans have brought that approach here in our day. So is it any surprise that USC has produced more Olympians than any other school?

Nikias praised them for choosing to attend a university intent on establishing the "platinum standard" for combined excellence in academics and athletics. He acknowledged that they faced extraordinary pressures as student-athletes at a university such as USC and cautioned that they faced extra scrutiny in a media capital such as Los Angeles. He urged them to make it their highest priority to grow in character and to display that character both when under the spotlight and beyond, "because character is destiny."

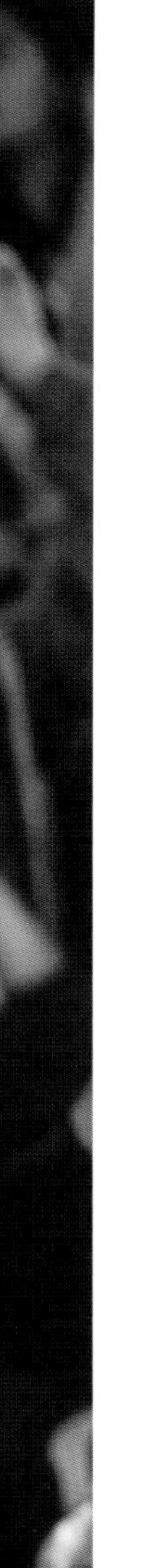

USC All-American quarterback Matt Barkley celebrates with fans after a historic, 50–0 victory over UCLA in 2011. Barkley, a rare four-year starter at Troy, led the football program bravely through some of its most challenging times. In 2009, he became the first true freshman quarterback in USC history to start in a season opener.

TOP: The president and first lady, a regular presence on the sidelines at Trojan athletic events, visit with USC's famed Song Girls.

BOTTOM: Football team captains Antwaun Woods (99), Anthony Sarao (56), and Cody Kessler (6) walk with game captain James Toland IV (26) to midfield for the coin flip before USC's contest against Utah in October 2015. The Trojans upset the third-ranked Utes, 42–24, in Clay Helton's first home game as interim head coach that year.

He also often spoke to them about taking a truly long-term view of their educational and sports careers. In his 2015 address, he told them:

> For USC, everything that we do—everything!—is done with an eye toward who you will be over the long course of your lifetime. Remember: Most of your life will come after your playing days. The crowds will grow silent as you grow older. Your life will then consist of what you have begun to build here—good relationships, good education, and above all a good reputation.

Trojan Marching Band director Art Bartner leads "the Spirit of Troy" in a 2015 lakeside rally in Chicago for the USC faithful before the team's matchup with Notre Dame in South Bend, Indiana.

By 2015, USC student-athletes enjoyed numerous resources not available to past generations of Trojans. The new and upgraded facilities provided a far higher quality and quantity of infrastructure. The vastly expanded compliance initiatives allowed the athletic program to navigate regulatory challenges and promote the university's core values within every sport. And new teams in sand volleyball and lacrosse added breadth to USC's competitive tradition.

The path was now clear, as Nikias had said in his 2010 inaugural address, to build a "Trojan heritage of student athletics that will be more glorious than before."

Hahn Plaza, the major pedestrian thoroughfare through the University Park Campus, received a dramatic makeover in 2011. A new fountain, red-brick walkways, and other flourishes gave the area the inviting visual signature of a European piazza in the Middle Ages. Today it serves as a symbol of the extensive beautification process of both USC campuses in the past five years.

Chapter 11

Campus and Infrastructure

USC's Rapidly Changing Landscape

What would the ideal university of the 21st century look like? A few decades ago, futurists imagined gleaming silver structures filled with technology inspired by science fiction. More recently, some experts predicted that the learning process would soon be unplugged forever from a physical setting, and that many traditional campuses would be shuttered. In contrast, USC's vision was that the campus would remain core to the university's purposes and activities. "Technology will enhance, but not replace the traditional USC environment," President Nikias said.

Accordingly, its leadership intensified efforts to build a university that embodied what was both most majestically timeless and thrillingly current in higher education. The goal was to maintain and refine a local environment that promoted the most elevated levels of scholarship and research, social and cultural interaction, patient care, and community service. Such a place would meld the ideals of beauty, communal spirit, and functionality within its boundaries.

Over the past five years, USC has broken ground on, constructed, and dedicated a host of facilities on both its University Park and Health Sciences campuses, adding academic capacity as well as an inviting aesthetic. In addition to numerous new buildings, ongoing beautification efforts expanded lawns and green areas, making them more lush and warm, with more than 700 trees and shrubs planted. Some older facilities were replaced with improved, larger ones, adding architectural style as well as functionality. And vanguard technology was built into the new and old structures alike.

When the Ronald Tutor Campus Center opened in the fall of 2010, the 192,000-square-foot facility immediately became the social center of gravity for University Park, offering students, faculty, staff, and alumni spaces to congregate, dine, and learn. Its immense Trojan Family Room welcomes in grand style throngs of visitors, many of whom are prospective students exploring their interest in applying to the university. Like other USC buildings built in recent

years, the Tutor Center is faithful to the resplendent Romanesque design of the school's original master plan while offering its own modern updates and state-of-the-art technologies on the inside. In 2014, the Garage—the major hub for the new Jimmy Iovine and Andre Young Academy for Arts, Technology and the Business of Innovation—opened within the Tutor Center.

USC's School of Cinematic Arts first reached international fame in an era when it was housed in a humble set of army barracks. But its renowned alumni and supporters—especially *Star Wars* creator George Lucas—have in

USC's world-renowned School of Cinematic Arts operated out of humble wooden bungalows a few decades ago. After the completion of a three-phase expansion plan, it now boasts facilities that would be the envy of many major studios.

The Ronald Tutor Campus Center became a primary crossroads for the USC community upon its opening in 2010. The grand, 192,000-square-foot facility, named in honor of Trustee Ronald Tutor's lead gift, offers space for dining, socializing, and university events of every size and scale.

recent years invested hundreds of millions to ensure that future greatness would be achieved in the best possible conditions. In 2013, construction was completed on the final two-year phase of the school's immense, state-of-the-art complex on the north edge of campus. Its interactive cinematic technologies set a formidably high standard to which its peer schools can aspire.

That year also marked the opening of the 101,000-square-foot Engemann Student Health Center, which represented a major enhancement of healthcare services for students, staff, and faculty on the University Park Campus.

The fall of 2014 saw the opening of two structures of visionary style and scope. Dr. Verna and Peter Dauterive Hall debuted that September as a major home for USC's faculty and students in the social sciences and professions. At a luncheon commemorating the opening, then-Provost Elizabeth Garrett said that it would spur "collaborative and interdisciplinary research in the social sciences that requires expertise across many fields and connections to translate the work into society."

The facility was designed with large community spaces in order to encourage serendipitous encounters of experts in various fields. Benefactor and longtime trustee Verna Dauterive spoke of feeling "deeply humbled and very excited about the building," adding that she looked forward to "what will happen inside—gifted bright stars working together to change the world in

wonderful ways that will create brighter futures for all societies."

A few weeks later, the university celebrated another milestone in the social sciences when it opened Wallis Annenberg Hall, a cutting-edge addition to USC's Annenberg School for Communication and Journalism. "It started with the idea that the real future of journalism—the students here—should learn and train and innovate in the kind of 21st-century newsroom, the kind of interactive, multimedia incubator, that should be commonplace in 10 or 15

The new Wallis Annenberg Hall, seen here from the rear, was designed to offer numerous settings in which students and faculty could convene, plan, collaborate—and connect with the news of the world. Upon entering the structure, visitors are greeted by a state-of-the-art, 30-foot digital media wall showcasing student programming in real time.

Wallis Annenberg Hall will allow students and faculty to define the future of journalism for a new digital era. The 88,000-square-foot building, featuring a combination of classical and contemporary styles, opened its doors in 2014. It was made possible by a $50 million gift from Trustee Wallis Annenberg.

years," Wallis Annenberg said at the dedication. President Nikias thanked her, USC's longest-serving trustee, for four decades of leadership and generosity and for her latest effort to "forever give students access to a world of exciting possibilities, where they will create and convey timeless stories that connect and chronicle the human journey."

In addition to these formal opening ceremonies, in 2014 USC also celebrated breaking ground on several important buildings on the University Park

TOP: USC's faculty and staff club was relocated to a majestic setting on the north edge of the University Park Campus. The new and expanded University Club at King Stoops Hall opened in the spring of 2012, following a half century at its former location near Town and Gown.

BOTTOM: The 101,000-square foot, state-of-the-art Engemann Student Health Center, made possible by a $15 million gift from Trustee Michele Dedeaux Engemann and her husband, Roger Engemann, opened in 2013 on the University Park Campus. The facility, which represented a crucial upgrade for a growing student population, also serves faculty, staff, and community residents.

USC's engineering quad, or "E-quad" for short, received a face-lift in 2013, creating an improved convening place for numerous academic and social activities that resulted in what one student blogger described as her "new favorite study space."

Campus, as well as on USC Village, the biggest real estate development in the school's history.

Construction began in April 2014 on the USC Glorya Kaufman International Dance Center, headquarters for the university's sixth independent arts school, the new USC Kaufman School of Dance. The facility, scheduled to open its doors in 2016, includes top-flight performance spaces; a variety of studios, classrooms, and collaborative areas; and a dance wellness center.

Hundreds of supporters gathered that September to celebrate the formal groundbreaking for Jill and Frank Fertitta Hall, a major building that will

TOP: USC broke ground on the Michelson Center for Convergent Bioscience in 2014, with a target completion date of 2017. The facility will be the largest building on the University Park Campus. USC officials intend for it to serve as a hub for a regional biotechnology corridor.

BOTTOM: The 60,000-square-foot Glorya Kaufman International Dance Center, opening in 2016, will house USC's sixth independent arts school, the Glorya Kaufman School of Dance.

Towering above the main entrance of the University Park Campus at Exposition Boulevard and Figueroa Street, Jill and Frank Fertitta Hall will provide a home for students and programs at the USC Marshall School of Business. It will expand the school's undergraduate student capacity by nearly a third.

house and support undergraduate business education. This majestic, modern yet classic structure will stand as the de facto gateway to University Park, at the corner of Exposition Boulevard and Figueroa Street.

The following month, October 2014, construction began on the USC Michelson Center for Convergent Bioscience. When completed it will be the largest building on the University Park Campus, as well as the possible foundation for a future biomedical research corridor of massive scale.

Just as USC asserts that it has entrepreneurialism in its DNA, the physical growth of its infrastructure reflects a certain strategic resourcefulness. The vast and spacious Dauterive Hall had previously been the site of a modest, one-story structure housing the USC University Club. The club was relocated,

Construction began in 2014 on USC Village, the largest development project in the history of South Los Angeles. Above, a team studies construction plans, with the USC Caruso Catholic Center standing behind them, just to the east of the building site.

When USC Village opens in 2017, it will add essential new services for the academic and local communities. It will also link University Park more closely to the vibrant and growing downtown Los Angeles area.

in 2012, to an underutilized space on the north edge of campus, in King Stoops Hall—where the larger venue became even more popular than its predecessor. Limited by necessity to about 230 acres, University Park nevertheless continues to grow in capacity, beauty, and even green space.

A Village Worthy of a Global Crossroads

In September 2014, the university joined with local and regional leaders and residents to celebrate the formal groundbreaking of USC Village, a $650 million project that may be the largest such development to date in south Los Angeles. President Nikias declared that, when completed in 2017, it would serve as "an inviting new town square for all members of our community." Speaking of its stately Romanesque design, he quipped that it would "instantly give our university and our city the distinguished appearance of a thousand years of history that we don't yet have."

USC Village will host nine residential colleges and add 2,700 beds for students, signaling that USC's decades-long transformation into a fully residential university is nearing completion. It will also bring popular retailers into the neighborhood to serve the students and faculty.

The grand scope of USC Village was appropriate, Nikias said, because

"our corner of Los Angeles isn't just another city neighborhood. It is a unique microcosm of the diverse new global society that is coming into being. It fully deserves an unsurpassed gathering place like this, which breathes an air that is both classical and contemporary into our great city."

A Medical Campus Makeover

The Health Sciences Campus had by 2010 increased its operations to draw a million visitors each year, and it would continue to grow, based on the university's plans to continuously expand its medical and healthcare enterprise. In the fall of 2011, the 120,000-square-foot 2001 Soto Street Building opened, remedying a space shortage on the campus; three years later, a structure at 2011 Soto added another 284,000 square feet of room to grow. In 2013, a lead gift by the Kenneth T. and Eileen L. Norris Foundation made it possible to begin construction on the Norris Healthcare Consultation Center, an important addition to the USC Norris facilities. And work began on Stevens Hall, a new home for the renamed Mark and Mary Stevens Neuroimaging and Informatics Institute led by Arthur Toga and Paul Thompson.

In 2014, the university broke ground on a mixed-use hotel with 200 rooms, and on a project to house 450 medical and graduate students. Construction also began that year on the Malcolm and Barbara Currie Residence Hall, a crucial new housing unit for students in the health sciences.

USC officials determined that a beautification program of monumental scope was both deserved and required. "We want our Health Sciences Campus to be just as beautiful and admired as our University Park Campus," Nikias said. At the outset of his presidency, he had announced that a verdant, green pedestrian network would soon connect the buildings and courtyards, with tree-lined and well-lit streets. USC rapidly began moving unsightly power lines underground, enhancing signage, and improving the walkways traversed by visiting patients.

"It was Christopher Marlowe who first said that the face—the beauty—of Helen of Troy could set in motion a thousand ships," Nikias said, quoting the English poet. "If the new face of our City of Troy can bring in a few thousand new patients, we'll be very happy!"

The Uytengsu Aquatics Center, upon its opening in 2014, gave USC a premier venue for its men's and women's intercollegiate swimming and diving teams and enhanced recreational and competitive opportunities for the larger academic community.

Reinforcing the Walls of Troy

For decades, USC's intercollegiate athletic heritage had been of a far greater caliber than the facilities that served its student-athletes, coaches, staff, and tutors. Many of the buildings where athletic excellence was nurtured hadn't been upgraded in a generation. In recent years, university leaders have made a concerted effort to remedy this situation in short order.

A number of donors stepped up in 2011 to provide the bulk of the money needed to build the John McKay Center, which would serve all 21 sports. Upon opening in 2012, it drew national attention for quickly transforming

USC's athletic facilities from a liability to a considerable asset in recruiting the world's best student-athletes. In addition to offering such boons as tripling the weight-room facilities and providing the football team with an indoor field, the McKay Center became home to the Stevens Academic Center, with dramatically improved facilities for counseling, studying, and tutoring.

Donors also paved the way for major renovations of Heritage Hall, the "mecca" of USC athletics, as well as significant improvement to the Uytengsu Aquatics Center and the Marks Tennis Stadium; the creation of sand volleyball courts; and the expansion of the Howard Jones Football Practice Field.

Bulldozers, concrete-mixing trucks, and construction zones had been a fact of life for the USC community for years, if not decades—long seen as noisy

symbols of continual growth and improvement. But by 2015, the university's infrastructure was approaching a new level of development. It had become clear that many predictions had been wrong: The traditional college campus was not going to be replaced by technology anytime soon, and in fact, the best universities would develop ever-better physical spaces for research, teaching, culture, patient care, and social life. The changes at USC hinted strongly at what the future would look like at other premier universities.

Every day, Trojan student-athletes pass through the All-America Walk, where the words “A Sound Mind and a Sound Body” are inscribed in Greek. The inscription was Athletic Director Pat Haden’s tribute to Nikias’s heritage—as well as the president’s belief that this all-encompassing ideal of the ancient Greeks should guide USC’s student-athletes today.

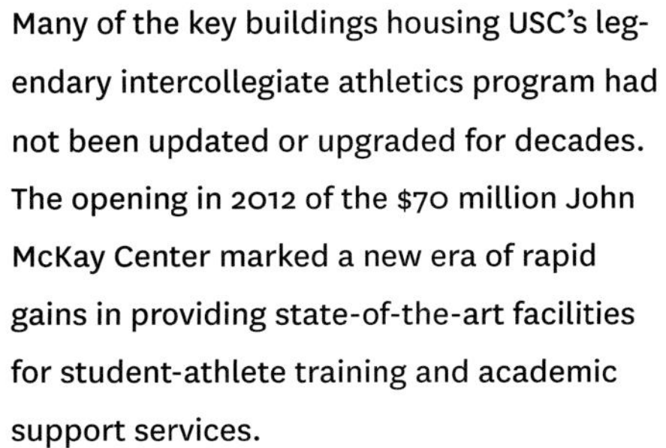

Many of the key buildings housing USC’s legendary intercollegiate athletics program had not been updated or upgraded for decades. The opening in 2012 of the $70 million John McKay Center marked a new era of rapid gains in providing state-of-the-art facilities for student-athlete training and academic support services.

New Infrastructure 2010–2015

More than two dozen major building projects have commenced at USC since 2010, transforming the landscapes of both the University Park Campus and the Health Sciences Campus.

OPENING 2017

USC Village
1,200,000 square feet
Groundbreaking 2014

Michelson Center for Convergent Bioscience
190,000 square feet
Groundbreaking 2014

Stevens Hall
45,700 square feet
Groundbreaking 2014

Marks Tennis Stadium
25,000 square feet
Groundbreaking 2015

OPENING 2016

Jill and Frank Fertitta Hall
102,000 square feet
Groundbreaking 2014

Glorya Kaufman International Dance Center
60,000 square feet
Groundbreaking 2014

Norris Healthcare Consultation Center
116,700 square feet
Groundbreaking 2014

Malcolm and Barbara Currie Residence Hall
264,000 square feet
Groundbreaking 2014

OPENED 2014

Wallis Annenberg Hall
86,000 square feet
Groundbreaking 2012

Dr. Verna and Peter Dauterive Hall
110,00 square feet
Groundbreaking 2012

"The Garage," Iovine and Young Academy
(at Tutor Campus Center)
Established 2013

Heritage Hall
71,700 square feet
Groundbreaking 2013

Uytengsu Aquatics Center
18,265 square feet
Groundbreaking 2013

IMAX Theater and Immersive Lab
(Addition, Robert Zemeckis Center for Digital Arts)
3,400 square feet
Groundbreaking 2013

OPENED 2013

Engemann Student Health Center
100,000 square feet
Groundbreaking 2011

School of Cinematic Arts
62,500 square feet
Groundbreaking 2011

2011 Soto Street Building
284,000 square feet
Groundbreaking 2012

Verdugo Hills Hospital
(Acquisition)
Acquired 2013

Town and Gown
Interior redesign
2013

OPENED 2012

University Club at King Stoops Hall
16,570 square feet
Groundbreaking 2011

John McKay Center
103,500 square feet
Groundbreaking 2011

Brain and Creativity Institute
(Addition, Seeley G. Mudd Building)
12,000 square feet
Groundbreaking 2011

Hahn Plaza
Hardscaping and redesign
2013

OPENED 2011

2001 Soto Street Building
120,000 square feet
Groundbreaking 2010

OPENED 2010

Ronald Tutor Campus Center
193,000 square feet
Groundbreaking 2008

Eli and Edythe Broad Center for Regenerative Medicine and Stem Cell Research
80,000 square feet
Groundbreaking 2008

President Nikias kicks off the annual *Los Angeles Times* Festival of Books at USC. This growing, multifaceted celebration formerly hosted by UCLA now gives USC the opportunity to showcase the beauty and resources of its University Park Campus to more than 150,000 visitors every year.

Chapter 12

The Closest of Neighbors

USC and Its City

USC was founded in 1880 to help fuel the development of Los Angeles—then a small village with a population of less than 12,000—into a major city with a distinct character. However, as a result of that very growth, university leaders a generation later would explore whether the school should move outside the city limits, in order to have more room to expand beyond the bustling metropolis.

Following these deliberations, however, in 1917 USC's fourth president, George F. Bovard, made a historic announcement. "There are two kinds of institutions, both of which have their place," he wrote. "One is the small college, placed by itself and sufficient to itself, with country surroundings and its campus remote from the city. The other is the city institution—the university which tries to solve the problems of the city."

USC, then, was to remain that latter type of institution. In the following decades, the question would occasionally arise as to whether the university would do well to relocate to more pastoral surroundings miles from the city center. Each time, its leadership reaffirmed the commitment of Judge Widney and President Bovard to be an anchor for Los Angeles. The civil unrest in the city in the early 1990s posed a challenge, as some experts warned that the region seemed unpromising for the recruitment of top students and faculty. USC's response was, characteristically, to focus on identifying and capitalizing on the distinctive advantages that were inherent in its setting, in the arenas of both academia and public service.

The university saw its location in southern Los Angeles as a prized asset for civic-minded scholars: Here lay countless opportunities to explore and improve a city that was a bellwether of urban change and a microcosm of a globalizing society.

Skeptics who believed the urban setting would be a drawback were consistently proven wrong. By 2015, USC ranked third nationally among private

The *Los Angeles Times* Festival of Books at USC features a health pavilion where members of the community can receive free medical screenings and consultations from university healthcare specialists.

Kicks for Kids, a USC student-run organization, helps local children with physical and developmental disabilities to live active and healthy lifestyles.

universities in applications for its freshman class. And a substantial portion of those applicants shared the belief of the greater Trojan community—that USC's place at the heart of Los Angeles represented an academic, cultural, and social treasure, as well as being an excellent location to begin a career.

A Growing Partnership with the Community

Over the years, USC has created hundreds of community partnerships, regularly drawing national acclaim. In their annual feature in 2000 on America's best colleges, *Time* and *The Princeton Review* named USC their "College of the Year" in recognition of the university's vast and innovative community service efforts. And USC typically stood at or near the top of the regular "Saviors of Our Cities" list—created to recognize schools that are the "best neighbors" in their urban settings.

Under President Nikias, the USC leadership doubled down on this culture of involvement. "A drive up Vermont Avenue does not simply show us a city. It displays to us the extraordinary span of the Pacific Rim, in microcosm," Nikias said in his 2010 inaugural address. "We will embrace this community as a unique social laboratory, within the context of our mission in education, social science scholarship, healthcare, and public service."

He would soon announce initiatives that would improve local K-12

education, create jobs and nurture area businesses, bring high speed Internet access to families, and expand key service programs to the neighborhoods surrounding the Health Sciences Campus. In just one example, USC committed $1 million to upgrade the nearby Hazard Recreation Center, which would include a jogging path, enhanced tennis and basketball courts, and exercise equipment. By 2015, the university was investing $35 million annually to support efforts that served 40,000 residents in the local area.

Student and Trojan Family Involvement

In an address to the student body in the spring of 2011, Nikias urged them to "celebrate the city"—to take advantage of the unlimited opportunities around

Some 200 community residents attend an event celebrating USC's $1 million gift to improve the Hazard Recreation Center near its Health Sciences Campus. The donation funded the addition of basketball courts, a gym, and a children's play area.

them to experience multiple cultures, to serve, to learn, and to grow.

"Even a few decades ago many Atlantic cities did not take L.A. seriously as a world city," Nikias told them, "until they realized that the fusion that you find here, from the arts and culture...to fashion and cuisine and commerce, reflects something difficult to imitate elsewhere. Increasingly, others appreciate how Los Angeles is so breathtakingly open to change, to reinvention, to forward-thinking...and to possibilities without limit."

While many urban universities are emotionally divorced from their surroundings, USC's faculty, students, and staff are personally involved. By 2015, almost two-thirds of undergraduates were volunteering and staffing the university's myriad service programs, including a remarkable 650 student-athletes who found time to give back to local schools, hospitals, and institutions. Combined, USC's employees and student body now offer more than 650,000 hours in service every year.

The Trojan Family's commitment goes beyond volunteering. USC's Good Neighbors Campaign allows its employees to contribute directly to partnerships between the university and its neighborhoods. Annual giving by faculty and staff rose from an impressive total of just under $1 million in 2007 to $1.6 million by 2015—by which time, some 450 employees were giving at least 1 percent of their income to the efforts funded through the campaign.

Local Economic Development

In the university's public-service priorities, economic development goes hand in hand with other local efforts. Through just one initiative, the academic community worked to help 60 small business owners develop the skills needed to procure some $61 million in working capital, loans, and contracts. In another example, a nearby hiring program was able to put $5 million in USC salaries back into the local economy annually.

Celebrating the beginnings of USC Village (clockwise from top left): In December 2012, community members bedecked in USC cardinal colors show their enthusiasm for the proposal; Senior Vice President for University Relations Tom Sayles, who led USC's efforts to build support for the project, shakes hands with Los Angeles city councilmember Ed Reyes; hundreds of supporters cheer outside City Hall after the council approved the plans with a unanimous vote.

In 2013, the Los Angeles County Economic Development Corp. (LAEDC) recognized USC with an Eddy Award for its contributions to the region's vitality—as a research institution, for its longtime role as the largest private employer in the city, and for its plans to establish the $650 million USC Village, which would bring 12,000 jobs to the South Los Angeles area, 8,000 of which would be permanent.

The USC Village development, now underway and scheduled for completion in 2017, will create a vibrant retail and housing center in the heart of the campus. At a September 2014 groundbreaking ceremony, Nikias suggested the initiative was a sign of the interdependence of "town and gown" in the region:

For USC and Los Angeles to make the next step forward, there

was the need for this moment to come about. USC's first-rate faculty and first-rate student body need first-rate facilities. And Los Angeles needs its private university, its largest private employer, to be at its best…and at its most productive and influential. We recognized, together, how our community could receive a huge benefit from the new retail space, which could provide jobs and services to so many people locally.

USC's goals for enriching the area went beyond adding traditional jobs: They also included efforts to encourage development in emerging industries and sectors of the economy. In early 2015, Nikias convened a regional summit, drawing together scores of business, academic, and government leaders to

From current students to alumni, the Trojan Family remains committed to local service. As part of the annual Community Bowl, organized by the Trojan Athletic Parents Association, 150 student-athletes a year mentor local children and work alongside them to beautify their schools.

Retired judge James Reese graduated from the USC Gould School of Law in 1946, courtesy of the GI Bill. He worked with his alma mater to create Kinder 2 College, a unique program dedicated to ensuring that boys from disadvantaged backgrounds gain reading skills that are crucial to lifelong success.

advance a plan for a major biotechnology park in the area. This endeavor, he said, would potentially stimulate thousands of additional jobs, attract venture capital funding and new businesses, and unleash innovation.

A Community Crossroads

The *Los Angeles Times* Festival of Books has become an acclaimed literary gathering since its founding in 1996. For its first 15 years, the event was hosted by UCLA, which meant that more than 100,000 visitors from Southern California and across the nation would travel to its Westwood campus over two springtime days each year.

When budget cuts at UCLA compelled it to scale back its commitment to the book festival, USC leaders recognized that hosting the event could allow them to introduce the beauty, energy, and walkability of the University Park Campus to a sizable audience. The warmth of the ever-growing campus had long been a chief selling point to visiting prospective students and their families; the time seemed right to welcome even more outsiders. USC was also in a position to offer the organizers of the festival far more support and extensions than they had previously enjoyed. In the spring of 2011, the Festival of Books reappeared in the heart of Los Angeles, enabling USC to showcase its campus, as well as many of its best scholars, to some 150,000 attendees.

USC pledged an annual gift of $100,000 in 2014 to support the Los Angeles Police Department's cadet program. President Nikias regularly hosts and addresses the graduating classes of cadets.

Trojan tight end Chris Willson rallies the troops during a visit by several USC football players to 186th Street School in 2015.

USC organizers also helped coordinate a dizzying array of programs, panels, workshops, lectures, and other events—some 100 in total, spread across the 230-acre campus. The festival has expanded to become far more than a literary showcase, now including a variety of musical, culinary, and cultural offerings, as well as health screenings and community services. The Southern California and literary communities warmly embraced the new location of the expo, which emerged as the biggest of its kind in America, as well as one of the most admired. "This gigantatron gathering of readers, authors, book sellers, panelists, artists, and literary experts is one of the best known anywhere," gushed one review from NBC online.

In another sign of commitment to its local neighborhoods, USC took under its wing those entrusted with keeping the city secure, hosting commencement ceremonies for the LAPD Cadet Leadership Program. President Nikias regularly delivered keynote addresses to the graduating cadets. In 2014, USC pledged a $100,000 annual gift to support the growing youth academy.

"This support speaks to USC's confidence in these young women and men, and our shared commitment—along with LAPD—to our community and its youth," Nikias said in announcing the award. "These cadets are our future. Look at them. It's America's future," he said. "The USC community stands with them, not only today but every day for the many years to come."

School Is In: Expanding Educational Opportunities

Just as education is at the core of USC's overall priorities, it remains a cornerstone of the university's community service work. A crucial component involves improving K-12 learning opportunities for children attending nearby schools. By 2015, as part of its Family of Schools initiative, USC had "adopted" 15 neighborhood elementary, middle, and high schools, freely sharing its extensive educational resources. More than 3,000 local students were enrolled in a variety of college access programs, as well as more than 500 children in preschool offerings.

The Neighborhood Academic Initiative (NAI) also has emerged over the years as a signature USC effort in K-12 preparation. More than 800 students

RIGHT: President Nikias visits students at the James A. Foshay Learning Center, part of the USC Family of Schools. The university currently partners with 15 local schools through the program to enhance education for more than 17,000 young people, with participation from some 4,500 Trojan students, faculty, and staff.

in the University Park area have successfully completed the program since its launch in 1991; it boasts a 99-percent success rate in graduating its participants from high school and sending them off to college. Those who manage to earn direct admission to USC enroll as freshmen the next fall, supported by full-expense scholarships; other NAI students have gone on to attend Harvard, Penn, and West Point, among other schools. In a typical year, a few dozen young people who, without NAI, may have been challenged to finish high school at all, find themselves able—and equipped—to attend one of the nation's most prestigious private universities. Many participants who have graduated from USC return to the program as volunteers, to mentor a new generation of scholars and coach the students' parents.

In 2014, a record 65 high school seniors graduated from NAI. The following year, Trustee Joan Payden made a landmark $5 million donation that would dramatically expand the range and scope of the program's academic services. The gift enabled NAI to serve an additional 600 schoolchildren from the neighborhoods surrounding the Health Sciences Campus, and also established the Joan A. Payden Student Academy.

Extending the Trojan Family

In the end, USC's efforts are driven by a public-service ethos rarely seen even at the nation's historic land-grant public institutions. And essential to that ethos is a belief in the power of family: The Trojan Family needs to be broad and open, creating as much opportunity as possible. The success of its community endeavors is exemplified by the story of Isidra Nava Garcia, a mother who has been involved with NAI for years. In 2014, she celebrated the graduation of her third child from the program; all three siblings will be studying at the university concurrently. "We will always be part of NAI," she said. "We are a USC family."

LEFT: USC undergraduates run a program teaching civic engagement and entrepreneurship to local schoolchildren. A student at Lou Dantzler Preparatory Charter School eagerly participates in one session.

Since 2010, President's House has provided young Trojans with a home for the holidays. Every November, some 300 students arrive by bus from campus for a Thanksgiving dinner hosted by the entire Nikias family. For many international students, this is their first introduction to the American Thanksgiving tradition.

Chapter 13

A Changing University, an Unchanging Spirit

New Traditions

USC today is "only" 135 years old—a young soul, by the standards of America's earliest universities, and even more so in comparison to those learning institutions that arose in Europe nearly a millennium ago and still stand today. Within a few years of the school's founding, some distinct, venerable traditions had already arisen at USC—and its students, faculty, alumni, staff, and parents embraced them firmly from the start. The university's alumni, who were being unleashed annually to play leadership roles across Southern California society, quickly gained a reputation as one of the most powerful and loyal networks in higher education.

Today a spirit of tradition is at the core of the Trojan Family experience, though it is certainly a forward-looking spirit. As the community has grown in size and global scope, now with 350,000 alumni and countless friends and supporters spread around the world, a number of new traditions have also taken shape.

New Traditions for the Newest Trojans

A USC education is designed to be a powerful, defining personal experience, filled with varied academic and social rituals, that generates enduring feelings of loyalty and mutual support among its students, parents, and alumni.

When President Nikias took office in 2010, he believed that the undergraduate phase called for an initiation ritual of memorable scale and scope. With that came a spectacular transformation of USC's annual fall convocation and Welcome Week program for new students.

The ceremony had long been an indoor, evening function with modest attendance. USC turned it into a morning gathering in Alumni Park, in order to put it on the same footing as its grand graduation celebration. The reinvented event now kicks off with an academic procession of university officials and faculty, along with the incoming Trojans, wearing academic regalia (minus the

cap associated with commencement). The students are seated in the same sections, arranged by their schools, as they will be at their graduations four years hence. It is a powerful symbol of a mutual promise and expectation on the part of the students, their families, the faculty, and the larger Trojan community.

During the ceremony, the young people are formally inducted into the ancient yet dynamically enduring tradition of the academy. Each USC dean (even those representing schools without undergraduate programs) takes a turn welcoming the newest Trojans to the community of scholars, as do student leaders and faculty representatives.

In his 2010 address at the first of these reinvented convocations, Nikias

ROTC cadets prepare to participate in USC's annual New Student Convocation. In the fall of 2010, the event was expanded dramatically and moved from Bovard Auditorium to Alumni Park.

At the start of a new academic year in 2015, President Nikias offers the USC "V for Victory" salute to students on Move-In Day.

challenged the newcomers, whether they were studying the arts or sciences, to avail themselves of the incredible opportunities that were open to them for the next four crucial, life-shaping years. He exhorted them to become fluent in the language of imagination and possibility. And he called on them to develop themselves into citizens who could improve and bring honor to their communities and their world, likening their journey to that of a noble family of antiquity:

> Nearly twenty-two hundred years ago, the great Roman politician and philosopher Cicero sent his only son away to college. All of the wealthy and powerful families in Rome wanted to send their sons to Plato's famous Academy in Athens. There was only one problem. Cicero's son, Marcus, like many students of his age, was more interested in the social aspects of higher education. Let's just say that he was neglecting the great books in favor of having a good time.
>
> So Cicero wrote an entire book of letters to his son to remind Marcus of his responsibilities to himself, his family, and his society. In short, he wanted to remind his son of the principles that lead to an honorable life.

Cicero titled his book *On the Obligations of a Good Citizen,* or, in Latin, *De Officiis.* This was in fact Cicero's last book. Even as he wrote it, he was aware that his opposition to Mark Antony might tragically end his life. Let me share with you some brief thoughts that Cicero hoped would be meaningful to his son, and that I hope might inform your days at USC.

What, Cicero asks, distinguishes a man from a beast? Animals are moved only by their senses, and cannot perceive the past or the future. Humans, on the other hand, possess a unique ability to reason and to comprehend the chain of consequences, perceive the causes of things, and connect the present and the future. A man, Cicero wrote, "can therefore easily survey the course of his whole life and make the necessary preparations for its conduct."

So, to paraphrase Cicero: The choices you make today will shape the person you become tomorrow. The actions you take in the present will have consequences in the future. Use your reason to make honorable decisions—decisions that will benefit you, your family, and your society. Cicero also tells his son, "We are not born for ourselves alone. We do not live for ourselves alone. Our country, our friends, have a share in us."

During Welcome Week, a Trojan father and mother share a letter they just wrote with their daughter. The Office for Parent Programs created this new tradition; the parents' letters are usually delivered to students during their first week of classes, although some families choose to share them in person.

Nikias concluded in a lighter vein by showing USC's newest Trojans how to make the "V for Victory" salute, so that they could greet their peers throughout the world with that universally beloved sign.

Carrying the same hopes that Cicero did two millennia earlier, parents became a more integral part of the revamped convocation. They gathered early for breakfast in the adjacent McCarthy Quad, then cheered for their children during the event. At the conclusion of the ceremony, the students processed out of Alumni Park, symbolically marking the ritual of separation, whereby the young people move into their independent, adult journeys.

By 2015, the convocation tradition had been expanded to the spring semester as well, so that USC leaders and faculty could greet and commission midyear enrollees. The spring program involved a Thursday night social mixer,

a Friday morning ceremony in Bovard Auditorium, and a subsequent reception in the Tutor Center.

As a part of his larger effort to expand the Trojan Family to include all parents, Nikias emphasized that the convocation and Welcome Week activities were not just a rite of passage for students but for their mothers and fathers as well. During Welcome Week, parents would take time to write letters to their children, which USC staff would later deliver to the students once classes began. And parents would be invited to reunite with their progeny several weeks later on Trojan Family Weekend, which would allow them to feel even more connected to the life of their children's university.

Immediately upon taking office, President Nikias began a tradition of meeting regularly with small groups representing a cross section of the student body. At these "student teas," attendees are invited to share candidly both what they enjoy about USC and what they feel could be improved.

First Lady Niki C. Nikias (center) expanded the annual Ladies' Tea event in order to allow full participation among local women's organizations that support the USC mission.

Honoring a Great Milestone in the Great Voyage

Through its convocation for incoming freshmen and transfer students, USC emphasized the nature of the academic journey upon which they were about to embark. For its commencement ceremonies, which represented the culmination of that academic journey (or at least the completion of a major chapter), the university's leadership fittingly introduced a charge from *The Aeneid*, Virgil's epic about the great journeys and destinies of the mighty Trojans. The passage was read in English, Latin, and the original ancient Greek.

> *My comrades, hardly strangers to pain before now, we all have weathered worse. Some god will grant us an end to this as well. You've threaded the rocks resounding with Scylla's howling rabid dogs, and taken the brunt of the Cyclops' boulders, too.*
>
> *Call up your courage again. Dismiss your grief and fear. A joy it will be one day, perhaps, to remember even this. Through so many hard straits, so many twists and turns our course holds firm for Latium. There Fate holds out a homeland, calm, at peace. There the gods decree the kingdom of Troy will rise again. Bear up. Save your strength for better times to come.*

Connecting at Teatime

In 2011, Monish Tyagi, then the president of the undergraduate student government, told the *Daily Trojan* that he was especially impressed by President Nikias's accessibility. "In the midst of all of the things he has to do and the demands in his schedule—the fact that he has time to engage with students speaks a lot to [his character]," Tyagi said. "He hosts monthly teas where he interacts with students, meets with our student government a few times a semester, and he is very student-friendly."

Immediately upon taking office, President Nikias had instituted a regular, monthly slate of "student teas," giving him the opportunity to engage with small cross sections of USC's undergraduates and graduates, who represent every walk of life and academic field.

The first lady welcomes attendees of the 2012 USC Women's Conference. Mrs. Nikias actively supports organizations that nurture academic and professional growth among the university's female students and alumnae.

Nikias described the teas as "sustain and improve sessions." He would begin by asking attendees to respond in their own way to the two-pronged question, "What do you believe needs to be sustained at USC, and what do you believe needs to be improved?" The insights he gained in these intimate conversations often found their way into the deliberations of his presidential cabinet, trustee committee meetings, and other official leadership discussions.

Jihyun Shin, a PhD candidate in international relations, participated in one tea session in 2014. As she later shared in a university newsletter, "President Nikias listened intently and took notes as we spoke.... During the meeting, I realized I had enjoyed all of these blessings without much reflection on how they developed. Like with every great achievement in the world, the things I love about USC do not arise on their own, nor are they sustained on their own. There are always people working behind the scenes and striving for greatness. The great things about USC are like the fruit that seems effortless, until you realize that it was the result of people's hard work and sweat."

Bridging Town and Gown

As one of her many new priorities as first lady, Niki C. Nikias dedicated herself to connecting with and building up the women of Troy. She participates in the USC Women's Conference, an annual offering of the Alumni Association to promote leadership, professional development, wellness, and financial strategy—some years giving the opening remarks. She has also reestablished and expanded the old tradition of hosting an annual Ladies' Tea at President's House, bringing together and honoring the many women's organizations that have long histories of raising millions of dollars each year to support the university.

USC unveiled a statue in 2014 honoring Judge Robert Maclay Widney, the man who, as President Nikias said, "moved heaven and earth" to establish a great university that could power the progress of a small but growing village in 1880.

The first lady also serves as the honorary president of Town and Gown of USC, the school's longest-running support organization. At its 2013 annual benefit, Town and Gown recognized the efforts of both the president and the first lady to promote arts and culture at USC and in the larger community. It commended Mrs. Nikias for her work in welcoming visiting artists into the university through a range of receptions, dinners, and other events, as well as her championing of the highly successful Visions & Voices initiative in the arts and humanities.

Beginning in 2010, USC significantly expanded its annual New Student Convocation, instituting a formal processional in which students would sit in the same sections reserved for their graduation ceremony four years later. Visible in the front row of the 2015 event are Texas governor Greg Abbott, First Lady Niki C. Nikias, and Trustee Steven Spielberg.

Campus Truly Becomes Home

By 2014, USC had established a new tradition as a residential university, one that housed all freshmen on campus during their crucial, formative first year. This followed years of planning and expansion at a university that was once viewed by many as a commuter school. And like so many other areas in which the university sought to grow, one part of the equation involved catching up to institutions who were leaders in the area, while the other part involved building USC's own leadership niche by capitalizing on certain advantages: in this case, the Trojan school spirit and camaraderie, and its prime location in the heart of Los Angeles.

The construction of the grand USC Village will add nine residential colleges upon its completion in 2017, each with faculty masters to help curate and steward undergraduates' round-the-clock living-and-learning experience. With the 2,700 undergraduate beds that the project will add to USC housing, the university will finally be able to turn 1,400 other beds north of campus into much-needed housing for graduate students.

Paying Tribute to a Tradition of Support

USC has always paid special tribute to contributors who make donations of historic size—some even reaching eight or nine figures. In 2012, however, the administration launched a tradition to honor all those who have given $1 million or more to the university in their lifetimes with the establishment of the USC Widney Society. Named in honor of the school's forward-thinking founder, Judge Robert Maclay Widney, the organization now annually inducts its new members at a gala held next to Widney Alumni House. Each inductee goes home with the society's symbol—an impeccably reproduced feather quill pen from the founder's era.

Caring for the (Entire) Trojan Family

In truth, every major American research university is a vast, nonprofit enterprise that relies on productive and mutually generous relationships. An eager, committed, and hardworking Trojan Family was the guiding metaphor of the new USC leadership's hopes of quickly moving the university forward. Therefore a key role of the incoming president and first lady was working to expand and deepen the bonds connecting 350,000 members of that worldwide community.

In their first five years in office, the Nikiases hosted or attended more than a thousand events—academic, cultural, athletic, social, and philanthropic—that brought together tens of thousands of members of the Trojan Family. The couple, who have been together for four decades, understood when they embarked upon the presidency that they would be booked most evenings in the cause of university business. Much of that business involved a constant practice of building community—and of caring for the people who care the most for USC.

Niki C. Nikias took on the role of chief caretaker of that Trojan Family. USC professor and renowned historian Kevin Starr told *Trojan Family Magazine*, "First ladies project the values of the university, and Niki is projecting something of USC's character—in the sense of an ambition to do things better, to make the world a better place." He added that it helped that she could do all this while exuding "empathy, optimism, and panache."

First Lady Nikias has said that gratitude for the blessings of education, and an attendant sense of stewardship, is what drives her. "Both Max and I were very fortunate," she told a reporter. "Our parents started from having nothing, and they built their own small businesses. Max's father was a carpenter, and he opened up his own workshop. My father was a clearing agent for importing goods in Cyprus. So we come from families who were very loving and very business-successful."

Her appreciation of her family has been equaled by her appreciation of her adopted nation. "It's only here in America where you come and you work hard and you succeed to achieve your goals," she said. "I mean, who would have dreamed that Max would be a president? It's been a great journey."

Mrs. Nikias was dedicated to ensuring that the next generation would have maximum access to education. She herself earned a bachelor's degree in accounting from the Athens University of Economics and Business in Greece and an MBA with a specialization in finance from SUNY Buffalo. She spent years as a corporate accountant and finance consultant in Athens, London, and the United States before taking leave to tend to her growing family.

@USCPRES ON INSTAGRAM: President Nikias dove into social media with both feet, launching his Instagram handle in 2014. With hundreds of posts and thousands of followers, @USCPres gives the Trojan Family around the world a window into his personal experiences and up-to-the-minute insights on USC events.

TOP ROW, from left: The president snaps selfies with actor Sylvester Stallone and his wife, Jennifer; music producer Quincy Jones; musician and global activist Will.i.am of the Black Eyed Peas; actor Pierce Brosnan; and comedians David Spade and Dana Carvey.

BOTTOM ROW, from left: First Lady Niki C. Nikias with Sandra Bullock and George Clooney; the president with Halle Berry; Will Farrell joins the Nikiases to cheer on the Trojan football team; and the president with Steve Carell.

Daughters Georgiana and Maria went on to distinguish themselves academically, both attending USC, pursuing multiple degrees, and moving into careers in law and journalism, respectively.

Upon becoming first lady, Mrs. Nikias suddenly saw her family grow to enormous size, but she brought the same principles to caring for the larger Trojan community. "I don't think I realized what the Trojan Family meant until I started spending more time at USC and getting involved with the different aspects of the university. Then I realized that it's like my own family, except that it's bigger."

Our Home Truly Is Your Home

The Nikiases took several intentional steps to make their new house the de facto home for the entire Trojan Family. They personally host approximately 50 to 60 university events a year at their official residence in San Marino, President's House.

A 2014 *San Marino Outlook* feature on USC's first couple highlighted the ease with which they carry out their duties, noting that they have hospitality "embedded in their DNA." The article reported:

"In Greek culture, you never sit down to have dinner alone," Niki

says. "There's always the neighbor, the cousin, the mother-in-law, the father-in-law who will drop by and say, 'Well, what's up for dinner?' And you don't even plan on it. Not only that, but you also plan a lot of parties—birthdays, celebrating by hosting dinners at the house. It's something that I've done a lot."

"The rule is," Max adds, "you don't do it unless you really love it. The pressure is always there, the time commitment is always there. The challenge you face is how you pace yourself. But

President and First Lady Nikias welcome guests to President's House in San Marino, adjacent to the famed Huntington Library and gardens. In preparation for the *Fas Regna Trojae* fundraising campaign, the Nikiases dramatically escalated the number of university events held at their official residence.

The Nikiases—often joined by their daughters, USC alumnae Maria (at left) and Georgiana—enjoy hosting thousands of Trojan Family members each year, especially during the busy holiday season.

> when you have to be on, you have to be on, and you have to love it. You can't fake it."

The article noted they insist on jointly greeting every single guest warmly at their front door—even if the event is a massive tented party of 400 people in their backyard. "It doesn't matter the size of the party," Trustee Lorna Reed told the *Outlook*. "When you walk in the door, they're both right there to greet you. Large or small, they make you feel you're the most important guest to walk through that door." Their welcoming policy meant that, in just their first four years in office, each of them shook about 15,000 hands at their home's entry, pausing to connect in a meaningful way with each member of the Trojan Family, as well as community leaders and other supporters.

A Trojan Family Dinner

In the fall of 2010, just a few months into the Nikias presidency, the Thanksgiving holiday was approaching, along with a rare chance for the president and his family to retreat from formal functions. Instead, the Nikiases determined, along with daughters Georgiana and Maria, to throw open the doors of President's House to some 250 "Thanksgiving orphans"—USC students who weren't able to return to their homes in other states or nations for the holiday. Buses delivered them from University Park Campus to San Marino, where they were given a traditional meal and a chance to learn more about the meaning of family—Trojan-style.

"We decided, as a group, that it was important for us to spend the holiday with USC's students," Mrs. Nikias said. "Max and I had been international students ourselves years ago, so we identified with what it felt like to not have family to be with on Thanksgiving Day. So we chose to bring them into our own family for the day. Being parents, Max and I feel like all these kids are our kids. It was beautiful to see the students filling their plates and coming up to us and saying, 'Oh, thank you. It was so great, so delicious.'"

"There's nothing like a home-cooked meal," Georgiana told the *Daily Trojan* in 2010. "Thanksgiving is a time to enjoy a really good meal, sit down, and be lazy. You don't do any homework; you just relax."

"We love the company," her younger sibling, Maria, added. "We know how important food is—good food—on Thanksgiving."

The generosity did not go untested or unappreciated. "Dinner was amazing," USC senior Sunit Rohant told the newspaper, adding that the event made one of the school's great claims—the existence of an intensely supportive Trojan Family—undeniable to him and other students. "I'm really glad that [President Nikias] invited all these students here because it just reinforces the idea of the Trojan Family, where we're actually having a family dinner together on Thanksgiving," Rohant said. "We went around in a circle and said what we were thankful for, and it just reinforces it."

The Thanksgiving dinner has become a regular event, growing to more than 350 students—some of whom even skip or cut short their own family celebrations so that they can join in this special Trojan Family holiday tradition.

Each year, hundreds of USC students gather at President's House for a Thanksgiving dinner hosted by the university's first family. Attendees include students from other states and countries—and even some local ones who trade in time with their own families on the holiday to be with members of the Trojan Family.

Supporting Troy's Warriors

During the first two years of their presidency, while the football team was under NCAA sanctions and therefore not eligible for a bowl game, the Nikiases made it a point to show their support for these athletes. As the president had noted in speeches to the USC community, the members of the 2010 and 2011 teams "inherited adversity, and they handled themselves with courage and class." One expression of their appreciation was hosting holiday celebrations

for the football team and its coaches and staff during these years at President's House. *Trojan Family Magazine* reported on one of the gatherings:

> One holiday guest, USC star quarterback Matt Barkley, says, "I sat next to Mrs. Nikias at the banquet, and we pretty much talked the whole night about traveling, Europe, and academics and other things." He adds, "It's always fun to talk to her, because of the way she conducts herself—very gracious, very welcoming and warm."

The first lady also brought her hospitality to the campus to support Trojan athletics. During the week of the USC-UCLA football game, it had become an annual practice for the Trojan Knights organization to stand guard over

USC
20 13
SWIMMING
& DIVING
SUPER BOWL
CHAMPIONS
USC

President and First Lady Nikias cheer on the Trojan football team at nearly every game—not only at home in the Coliseum but also at away games across the full breadth of the nation, from Boston to Hawaii.

Tommy Trojan, camping out each night to prevent meddling Bruins from defacing USC's beloved statue and icon. Mrs. Nikias began her own tradition, personally delivering classic Greek baklava to the Knights as they stood watch over the walls of Troy.

Athletic Director Pat Haden noted with admiration how the first lady took to her role with enthusiasm. "She really appreciates what the football game means to the Trojan Family. She's embraced that. She comes to all the games, home and away."

The Personal Touch

Mrs. Nikias is keenly aware of the demands of the presidency—as well as the opportunities to strengthen relationships with supporters, public officials, civic leaders, parents of students, and other key groups. Accordingly, the first lady does far more than simply show up at university events; she works long hours alongside the USC staff beforehand, learning about the individual guests and their interests, and then guides and directs each function so that attendees come away with deeper connections to the university.

Describing her role as "promoting USC through all its constituents and all the organized events," she has said, "There's so much to be accomplished, and this $6 billion fundraising campaign…is the key to how we want to bring USC to the next level. So we are really focused on that, and it takes a lot of our time."

Her efforts have drawn notice and praise throughout the university community. Calling her a "toughie," Board of Trustees chair John Mork told *Trojan Family Magazine*, "I've been on arduous, long trips with her—travel and miserable 14-hour days....She can hang in there with you. There's this warmth and calmness about her. When the whole world is spinning, she's there going, 'Oh, don't worry. We've got this.'"

During the high-intensity rivalry week leading up to the annual USC-UCLA football game, members of the Trojan Knights camp out night and day at the feet of Tommy Trojan to protect it from pranksters. To thank the Knights for guarding the university's famed symbol, First Lady Nikias brings them baklava, a family favorite.

Students from the USC Thornton School of Music perform holiday standards at a party for university faculty at President's House.

Gayle Garner Roski, alumna and Roski School benefactor, recalled being on an exhausting trip across India in 2011 as part of a high-level USC delegation working to establish key partnerships in the rising economic giant. "I saw Max and Niki going 24 hours a day, together, hand in hand," she said. "I love that about them. I'm always seeing Max pick up her hand, and I see how much she means to his life."

One of the annual events hosted at President's House is the dinner for the President's Leadership Circle of the USC Good Neighbors Campaign. Membership in this group is reserved for the hundreds of staff and faculty who contribute 1 percent or more of their salary to the university's community partnerships. The first lady has brought global variety and flair to these gatherings, instituting a different theme each year and representing the various ethnic cultures that make up Los Angeles's polyglot society.

Mrs. Nikias has drawn praise for her ability to bring a personal touch to such large-scale USC events, but many have noted that her true gift in building connections and relationships is even stronger in small get-togethers, where attendees can receive the full attention and warmth of the first couple.

This "hospitality gene" has led to new opportunities across the university. USC deans, for the first time, have been able to organize intimate dinners of 6 to 16 guests at President's House for key supporters and donors. The Nikiases host some 25 such development dinners each year. The first couple also regularly give small dinners for USC VIPs, civic leaders, and others important to the university's mission. President's House had traditionally hosted six holiday parties each year for faculty, supporters, and student leaders. In short order, the Nikiases doubled the number of these events, allowing hundreds of Trojans to join in the celebrations.

The 2014 *Outlook* feature noted that the Nikiases were willing to share their home and their time—particularly if it meant that the recipients of that generosity would in turn be more generous to USC:

> Niki asked that a bedroom suite be created on the ground floor. Max says he "half-jokingly, half-seriously" refers to it as the Lincoln Bedroom, because an overnight stay in those quarters costs $1 million, "payable to USC."

Guests stay up late chatting with their hosts and have breakfast with them in the morning. The couple still chuckle about the overnight visit of David and Dana Dornsife, who donated $200 million to USC's College of Letters, Arts and Sciences, which now bears their name. After breakfast the next morning, Max had to get to his USC office but told the Dornsifes they were free to linger and stroll the property. He chuckled at the memory: "I got a text from Dana: 'Thank you, Max, we had a great time; 199 nights to go.'"

Niki C. Nikias organizes and prepares for one of many university functions held at President's House each year. Intimate donors' dinners and small-scale entertaining have also become a part of the first lady's routine that has been noticed and appreciated throughout the community.

David Dornsife later said that over time, Mrs. Nikias had become the lynchpin of their relationship to the university. "Niki is one of my favorite people," David said. "We enjoy talking to the Nikiases, so a lot of times we'll arrive early to an event. That gives us a little bit of a chance to talk to her before the guests come in."

A Headquarters for Strategic Planning

The goal of the Nikiases has been to ensure that President's House remains "USC first" and only secondarily their residence. More than an elegant place for social and development gatherings, it has also served practical functions for

Rest, relaxation, and renewal: The Nikiases began a new presidential tradition of active cycling during their summer breaks, to let go of the pressures of the last academic year and prepare themselves for the rigors of the next one.

a variety of university purposes. Over the past five years, it has become the site of the annual board meeting for the USC Ming Hsieh Institute for Research on Engineering-Medicine for Cancer; it also played host to a number of retreats dedicated to campus planning and the development of USC Village.

The Nikiases occasionally managed, during their rare downtime, to return to their beloved house "down the road" in Rancho Palos Verdes, where they had raised their daughters, Georgiana and Maria, and felt most truly at home. "It's like a Greek island right here in California," Mrs. Nikias said. There they would unwind and find time to bicycle for dozens of miles to renew themselves.

They also vacationed occasionally at a home they purchased a few years earlier in picturesque Sun Valley, Idaho, where they might bicycle as much as 600 miles over a three-week period. But even the Sun Valley home became a place for the work of USC, serving as something of an unofficial Camp David, where the president conducted business and also hosted senior officers at an annual retreat prior to each new academic year.

Planes, Trains, and Automobiles: Taking the Presidency on the Road

While the president and first lady made their house a home for all the Trojan Family, the reality of the USC presidency is that the incumbents must also learn to live out of suitcases, crisscrossing continents to establish academic partnerships, recruit students and faculty, and cultivate support for the university's growth.

Yet even when far from home, the Nikiases have viewed their role as bringing others into USC's larger, worldwide family. At both the outset and the midpoint of the university's $6 billion campaign, they hosted thousands of alumni and supporters at "Trojan Family receptions" around the nation and overseas, encompassing southern and northern California, Dallas, Chicago, Boston, New York, and Washington, D.C.—along with visits to cities in Asia, Latin America, and beyond.

For the president and the first lady, the work of building the USC community never ends, but there is also no end to their dedication to the task. "Max loves what he's doing," said Mrs. Nikias, "and I love seeing him being happy. We don't see it as a job. With USC, it's a commitment. It's like your family."

President Nikias en route to another event in a grueling calendar that involves 80-hour work weeks and near-constant travel, all to build support for the university community and its academic mission.

Epilogue

What is the University of Southern California today? And can we say with certainty what USC is on its way to becoming within the next few years?

By the early part of this decade, higher education observers covering USC described it as a university aggressively moving forward. Some spoke of it seeking to become a "Harvard of the West" or a "Stanford of the South."

However, the university's leaders and most passionate supporters would argue that the goal isn't to emulate any other institutions, or even to compete directly with them. "There is no one else to chase now," President Nikias told the faculty in his annual address in 2013. "The university's goal now is to maintain its distinct identity and its distinct path, while accelerating the pace…all at a time when other universities are lagging due to economic constraints and other disruptions." To use an organic image, this would allow the school to come into full flower—to complete its own particular metamorphosis.

This will mean the university will have the intellectual, cultural, and social impact of the reigning elites—but in a manner fully characteristic of the University of Southern California that Judge Widney established in 1880 through unshakable determination and relentless effort.

Providence has placed USC in one of the most promising positions imaginable, as the United States' center of influence shifts steadily westward, and as the world's center of influence shifts rapidly toward the Pacific. West of Chicago, USC is one of only a handful of research universities of the first rank, institutions capable of nurturing economic and cultural progress. Among those institutions, USC and Stanford are the only two research universities that are both private, and broad and comprehensive (as opposed to being narrow technical institutes). Being independently governed, they are able to adapt quickly to new intellectual needs; and being comprehensive, they enjoy special opportunities to create meaningful interdisciplinary relationships.

But additionally, USC carries several other advantages that place it in a singular position going forward.

The university's academic community is especially national and global, with its student body representing all 50 states and 115 nations. It has long been home to more international students and alumni than any other university; and that global contingent is particularly notable, in that it includes an unrivaled number of the current and future leaders of the region that will dominate the next century—the Pacific Rim.

Los Angeles is emerging as the anchor city of the Pacific Rim and the chief hub connecting the United States to a Pacific future. And the USC community and its academic mission are already integrally and inextricably woven into the fabric of this great Pacific capital. As Nikias has told the

---

The Trojan Shrine—better known as Tommy Trojan—has stood sentinel at the heart of the USC campus since 1930.

faculty, "USC is finally in a position to capitalize on its strategic location—at the center of where the action will be in this century."

The Trojans' astonishing athletic and Olympic heritage symbolize its commitment to the classic ideal that the ancient Greeks saw as the broad pursuit of excellence in all things—in mind, spirit, and body, and in the building of communal spirit. Few of the world's top universities demonstrate this at the highest levels, and USC is becoming a model.

While USC has in recent decades achieved prominence in the traditional measures of quality at a research university, it also enjoys what Nikias has called its "secret weapon." The university hosts elite programs in engineering, the sciences, medicine, and other disciplines—but its secret weapon consists of six independent creative and performing arts schools, which together represent an unusual concentration of excellence in the arts and humanities. In another example of USC's commitment to an integrated approach to pursuing excellence, it has positioned its arts schools to supply the larger academic community with an infusion of creative energy. And this will increasingly nurture breakthroughs in the sciences and social sciences, technology, and the professions.

In his inaugural address in the fall of 2010, Nikias spoke loftily of how, "while USC imitates no one, I do believe USC has the chance to serve as an intellectual engine in this century, in much the way Oxford University emerged earlier as the intellectual engine of the British Empire and commonwealth nations."

If those words struck some observers as overly ambitious on that fall morning, they seem prescient today, based on the progress charted over the past five years. Bear in mind, however, that Nikias qualified his words with the phrase, "USC imitates no one." The Trojan Family represents a particular community of people with a distinct set of values. They seek not to replicate the successes of others, but to achieve their own successes, by staying faithful to their identity and to their forward-looking heritage.

The miraculous academic progress at USC in recent years required a willingness among its constituencies to step forward into the fog of uncertainty that characterizes our times, guided by some core principles and old-fashioned determination.

And so USC may be on course to completing a dramatic metamorphosis as an iconic 21st century global university—a development that would have seemed unimaginable to those who watched a tiny, local college on the Western frontier open its doors 135 years ago.

In that sense, USC's story is indeed a quintessentially American story; and its path increasingly seems likely to shape the story of America's emerging future in this still-new century.

Index

Page numbers in bold denote photos.

Credits

Production

Epicenter Communications
Dawn Sheggeby, Editorial Director
Tom Walker, Principal Designer
Matthew Naythons, President

www.epicenter.com

—

Brenda Maceo
Vice President for Public Relations and Marketing
USC University Relations

—

Sheharazad Fleming
Art Director
USC University Relations

Mary Modina
Project Manager
USC University Relations

—

Christian Camozzi
Director of Communications
USC Office of the President

Eric Ambler
Public Communications Coordinator
USC Office of the President

Printing

The Pace Group, City of Industry, California

Copyright

Photography

Dan Avila
Mark Berndt
Philip Channing
Benjamin Chua
Pierson Clair
Steve Cohn
Rose Eichenbaum
Eric Evans
Crystal Jiao
John McGillen
Tom Queally
Dietmar Quistorf
Tim Rue
Gus Ruelas
Chris Shinn
David Sprague
Van Urfalian
William Vasta

Additional photo credits

Karen Ballard, commissioned photography for *A Journey of Transformation*: Pages 40; 55; 62; 68 (far left, bottom); 69 (far right, top); 268; 273; 279
Page 90: Photo by Luis Sinco/Reuters
Page 102: Photo by Mark Boster/*Los Angeles Times*
Page 110: Photo by Alexander Mahmoud, Copyright Nobel Media AB
Pages 124-125: Photos courtesy of the White House
Page 126: Photo by Al Seib/Los Angeles Times
Page 135, second row center: Photo by Spencer Lowell / *WIRED* © The Condé Nast Publications Ltd.
Page 138: Photo by Anne Cusack/Getty Images
Page 164: Photo by Christine Cotter/*Los Angeles Times*
Page 197, top left: Photo by Larry Busacca/Getty Images
Pages 210-211: Photos by Ezra Shaw/Getty Images
Page 216, bottom left: Photo by Stu Forster/Getty Images
Page 217, top right: Photo by Alexander Hassenstein/Getty Images
Jacket, author photo: Marj Domingo, FotogGal Photography